BE READY TO DANCE WITH YOUR CUSTOMER!

HAPPY READING
+
GOOD LUCK

Shari Moss

Oct 7, 2019

# BE READY TO
# DANCE
## WITH YOUR
# CUSTOMER!

· · · · · · · · · · · · · · · · · · · · · · · ·

### HOW
## SOLID CUSTOMER SERVICE
### PUTS YOU AHEAD OF THE
# COMPETITION

· · · · · · · · · · · · · · · · · · · · · · · ·

## SHARI MOSS

BE READY TO DANCE WITH YOUR CUSTOMER!

*How Solid Customer Service Puts You Ahead of the Competition*

ISBN   978-1-61961-473-4   *Paperback*

978-1-61961-474-1   *Ebook*

LIONCREST
PUBLISHING

*To Kelly Gleeson, my stalwart enthusiast and champion of customer service, and to Philip Roy and Robb Gordon, for Beijing.*

# CONTENTS

..............................

# INTRODUCTION

..............................

entered the corporate world at the crux of a revolution. In the beginning, the working environment came in on the heels of Midtown Manhattan in the 1960s, but twenty years and twenty pounds older. If you haven't seen the show *Mad Men*, think martini lunches, cigar smoke-filled rooms, and men in suits dominating the field. It was the mid-eighties in Toronto, Canada. It was the land of one-car households, rudimentary television sets, and a single "real job" as it was called, more like Griswold than Draper. But things were about to change. And they were about to change in a big way.

A new generation was entering the workforce—a generation that I found myself swept up into. We were "DINKS," which stands for Double Income No Kids. Most lived with their significant other and so had access to a surplus of funds, and they came to be known as "Yuppies."

I was a Young Urban Professional, but, more importantly, I was a young woman entering a world that was essentially a man's in terms of the industry I was in and the product I was selling. In simple terms, I was selling basic wire and cable to manufacturers of everything from the toaster on your kitchen counter to the transformers that connect your home to the electric grid, to customized ambulances and the digital switching equipment that allows you to make calls across the continent. You get the idea.

At the time, the typical salesmen (the loud, gregarious, joking, happy-faced type of men) sold their wares primarily by entertaining their buyers. This meant a lot of alcohol-infused lunches, slaps on the back and, "good-old-boy" type of talk. And I will skip what was usually on the agenda for the evening's entertainment. It was a mutually beneficial relationship, at least for all parties that attended those lunches. I certainly never heard anyone complain!

But, to someone like me, working quietly in the background, I felt as though there was a true lack of something very important in this seemingly symbiotic relationship. That thing, specifically, was shining customer service. The salesmen were taking their friendly relationship with their buyers for granted; they were getting too comfortable, and thus they were getting lazy. They weren't really watching what was going on behind the scenes; they weren't watching me.

I did not appear to be a threat, of course. I worked simply

for a distributor, so my job was to stock the product. But I knew that as a middleman (which all salespeople are), the main job is to make sure that your customer service is unparalleled or that, at least, you can help to make your clients' businesses run smoother. Otherwise, companies like Northern Telecom could save themselves a lot of money and simply buy direct from the manufacturer, skipping the middleman-salesperson in the process. Companies do not always deal direct, as they don't necessarily want to stock and hold the inventory, manage it, and pay for everything upfront. Therefore, my job as a distributor was to order and manage their required product, stock it locally so when needed it was only a day away, take orders (learning for myself how their RFQs worked was a big advantage), ensure quality control was done, ensure the correct products were properly being sent to the correct locations, follow-up with customers, and, most importantly, make sure that customers were satisfied.

I had full access to our customers, so I started reaching out to them to make sure that they were fully satisfied with our business. There is a lot to learn in a big industry such as I was in, and so while the salesmen were on their extended lunches, I spoke to our clients' purchasing departments. It didn't matter who answered the phones; I spoke to everyone and anyone. Through them, I gained a lot of knowledge about who was important on the production floor, in quality control, on the managerial level, and in the buying department.

It was tough to get this type of information, but I found that it could be done. Eventually, I became really good at it—being very professional notwithstanding. Once I could internally map out a company, I requested appointments with the employees. I walked the production floor with the production managers. I sat in the quality control manager's office. I talked and talked and shook many hands. I remembered people's names. I knew Jimmy Buffet in QC and Rod Stewart on the production floor. I talked with all related buyers and their support staff to find out what they wanted, what they were lacking, what they were disappointed with.

The buyers (usually stressed or at the very least busy under a constant litany from others bearing down on them to get product rolling "efficiently and profitably") always need somebody who can speak their language and understand their needs without them having to take the time to continue that dialogue themselves. In order to understand their language, I first learned everything I could about the product. I would often consult with our manufacturers to see what I could learn from them outside of what was standard. They were eager, of course, to provide such information. I was amazed at how willing they were to teach me at their expense, and they were happy that I was as interested as I was. We all benefitted from the relationships. Eventually, through the relationships I was building, I became a preferred customer. That meant that I was getting ahead of the competition.

How did I establish all of these crucial relationships?

I used a simple formula with everyone that I interacted with. I would ask them two questions. *What are your biggest problems, and what can I do to help solve them?* And then...I listened.

I couldn't solve all of their issues—I could sure try—but the solution wasn't necessarily the only thing they wanted. All they truly needed was for someone to listen. Customers always have something to say, and I was prepared to hear them out; by taking that time to really listen, I was automatically heads above the rest.

I used these methods with the employees of Northern Telecom, and eventually through trust and hard work and unrivalled customer service, they became an important customer of mine. I serviced many important locations across Canada and in Mexico, working together with the employees as a team.

The other salespeople who were out with the supervisor having a steak at one in the afternoon on a Thursday thought that their job was done, but little did they know that I was on the customer's production floor shaking hands, greeting people, taking names, giving out mine, and quietly making noise. Being "buddies" just wasn't going to cut it anymore in this rapidly expanding and increasingly competitive world.

At the first company that I worked for, I met a man (who would eventually become my husband, now ex) who taught me a great deal about sales, and together we left to work at another company in the same industry but much larger in terms of locations and staff and opportunities. There was a wonderful balance of both men and women now holding supportive and key roles. We controlled distribution on a national level and excelled at this because of all the relationships we had nurtured with customers and suppliers. We had great freedom at that company and were able to implement some of the customer service ideas that we had utilized previously. We were given precious time to refine our practices. All of this resulted in my becoming the top salesperson at the company.

I had proven myself very well, and at that point, the owner of the company sent me out to another province to talk with one of his struggling branches. He asked me to speak about how I was able to target the customer and how I was able to consistently deliver top customer service. I was fairly young still, and so the moment I walked into that conference room of approximately twenty sales staff (of all levels from order desk to outside sales), I knew that I was in for a challenge. In the middle of the ladies and gentlemen sat three bored men who greeted me with their arms crossed and feet up. Certainly not hiding their contempt, they started calling me "Natalie Wood," I realized pretty quickly what was going on and knew that I had to take control of the situation immediately. One of the three went out of his way to make it obvious in the first five minutes that he believed I had absolutely nothing to teach him, without even knowing me. Very. Big. Mistake.

So, because I am quick and because I have guts, I stood up, opened the door, and told him, "You are finished. You can leave now."

He was stunned, and he waited, not knowing if I was serious or not. Wondering if he had made a terrible mistake, which he had, he was clearly becoming very nervous.

So, I continued, "It is very clear to me that you're not going to benefit from this whatsoever, so you are excused." He looked at me, stood up, and walked out the door straight into the boss who then waited for an explanation as to why he had been sent out of the meeting. Needless to say, those remaining sat up and began to listen. The importance of this story will become very clear later in the book.

The very next day, I was asked to assist on some calls out on the road with one of their salesmen who had been struggling to keep pace. The salesman was very unhappy with my being appointed to assist him, and so he chose his most difficult clients for me to meet with. He spoke French, I did not, and so included clients who preferred to only speak French. This did not deter me. At our first appointment, as I approached the buyer, I saw a sign on his desk in English that said, "I eat salesmen for lunch." As soon as I sat down, the first thing I said to him was, "Well, I hope you've had your lunch already." It was quick and it was effective. It opened him up and relaxed him, which in turn allowed me to help him.

I turned what could have been a hostile afternoon into a productive one. I asked him my trademark questions: "What is your biggest problem, and what can I do to help?" I let him do the talking, and we worked together to solve some of the concerns. One of his more problematic issues of excess inventory they no longer needed was handled by offering to look at and perhaps move some of it for him. After all, we were a wire and cable distributor.

The buyer had a very good day. My co-worker? He challenged himself to rethink his own capacity. This was a pivotal moment in my career; it was a lesson for me too with respect to others in the dance—the working relationship between all of us within the company, which I will delve into in a later chapter.

These two instances confirmed that I had to work with my fellow employees, those above me and those below me, with the same level of respect and with the same practices as I do with my customers. Just as I did with them, I watched, listened, and learned. This took me a step further in my evolution.

In the early nineties, after three years at this new company, my partner and I realized that we were ready to set out on our own. We opened our own distribution business based on the principles that we had fine-tuned. We had come up with a unique way of servicing our clients, and they were very happy with us. We were so well trusted that we were even able to charge a small premium in order to pay for the expansive support systems that allowed for our great customer service. Not surprisingly, buyers were willing to pay that premium. This signified to us that our clients prioritized our customer service over the price point.

I further crafted my practice through my own diligence

and proud determination, but was mentored early on by my business partner. We met when we were both hired at the same company: he as a salesman, and I as a clerk. I soon found, however, that I had serious drive and serious balls and a great desire to become successful, as did he. I had the energy and the positivity, and I wanted to be challenged. My partner saw this in me, and so he moved me into the sales department. He started me in inside sales, which quickly led to a supervisory capacity. All the while, I was able to watch and learn from him, which was crucial in my development because he is the single most talented salesman I have ever encountered. He had the charisma, the intelligence, and the vitality to be successful, and so I modelled myself after that. As he moved up, so did I. He continued to challenge me and teach me, and soon I became his right hand. When he was offered a new job at that national company, he took me with him. We were a great team, and this dynamic is what led to our success when we went out on our own. Of course, we got some things wrong in the beginning. There was a lot of trial and error in my learning process. But we didn't give up.

I understood that I had so much to learn; there was so much that I didn't yet know, but I was open to new ideas and new concepts. I was ready and willing to learn, and that made the difference for my success. I had to talk to people, continually look things up in books, and actively seek out information. I never forgot all I had learned earlier while attending day workshops. I had taken as many as were offered to me. It was a different process back then. Today, young people entering the corporate world who have grown up in the technology age approach the process of learning in a different way. For them, accessing information is so easy, and so they expect learning to be instantaneous. They need to learn about WWII? They can go to Wikipedia and read an eight-sentence synopsis. They need to learn how to make a pitch deck? They can Google it and 250,000 hits are displayed on their screen in 0.51 seconds.

They expect to know it all and get all of the answers at a touch of a button, or at the swipe of a finger. Millennials have grown up waiting for nothing. Furthermore, everything in their world has been taken care of for them. This is the generation that was raised by parents who had the money and resources to make this happen for them. Millennials managed to find a way to want for nothing. They were given all the tools to succeed: laptops and phones that had access to all the information in the world (they mistakenly believe these were their creations), a college education, and the financial and emotional support of their parents. Everything has come to them. What they have created, however, is where exactly those tools are going and what they will do with them.

As the Millennial generation left the competitive (albeit not real world) world of collegiate academia and entered the workforce, they brought with them this entitlement. They don't necessarily understand "starting in the mailroom" like their parents and grandparents did. They want to become managers; they want to excel faster and go further than their peers. They are driven to own their own businesses, to become their own shopkeepers. To be there now. And they do bring with them a level of creativity and freedom and expressive openness far advanced of those earlier generations.

What do I mean by shopkeeper? It is my term for the owner, the manager, or the person who is ultimately responsible for a business that provides a service or product. It's what I see this Millennial generation wanting to become right from the get-go. But unless they're prepared ahead of time, and/or get very lucky (think Zuckerberg), it will not happen as fast as they want. The world simply doesn't work fast enough just because you want it to. You must make that happen.

I hope that this book can help Millennials while they wait for the world to speed up to their pace. While you are waiting, you should use this book to help prepare. The more prepared you are, the faster "it" can happen for you. Whatever "it" means to you, all success is reliant upon a select number of fundamentals. This book speaks to those necessary fundamentals for the success of you, your business, and your employees.

This is a book that is meant to be kept in your back pocket. It is a book that you should refer to whenever necessary. It is a book to share with friends and family, co-workers, cofounders, and employees. It is meant for those who are driven for success and for those who want to have the edge over their competition.

Older generations give Millennials a lot of grief, but do not be mistaken; the world that they have inherited is tough, competitive, and merciless. Therefore, they need every leg up that they can get. The leg up, as you will learn from this book, is dependent upon how well you, as a shopkeeper, as an employee, or as a founder, can engage and lock in your customers. And this is accomplished through impeccable customer service.

When someone wants to lose weight, he or she should eat less and exercise more. They should avoid processed foods and overly sugary treats. They should eat essential greens, good fats, whole grains, and lean protein, etc., etc., etc. Everyone knows this to be the correct formula for weight loss. So why doesn't everyone lose weight? It's because it is stressful and overwhelming to make sure that you are eating properly and exercising effectively. In the end, no one wants to exercise; they want to eat chocolate croissants and pizza and bacon burgers with fries. Thus the weight doesn't come off.

However, if you could afford to hire a nutritionist and a personal trainer, you would find a different outcome. These two hired professionals work for you in order to take the work and the stress of losing weight off of you. The nutritionist gives you a piece of paper with exactly what you should eat. The personal trainer shows you exactly what to do and draws up a lovely chart. The process becomes less stressful because all you have to think about is doing what your trainer and nutritionist tell you to do. You are guaranteed to make progress.

This is what this book will be for you; it will be your nutritionist and personal trainer. In plain English, this book will give you simple, common-sense steps and advice in order to help you to understand how to give the best service to your customers. No need to stress! You will have access to simple and cohesive information, so refer to it, fill out the worksheets, underline and highlight freely, absorb it, and you will succeed. Most importantly, I want you to make this book your own.

As we move through the book, you will see that providing

great customer service is a dance. When done correctly, there is a rhythm, a flow—it has movement. It requires patience, a give and take, and a certain level of humility to mess up and keep going. It also requires the ability to listen and to take advice from someone who has been doing it for a long time.

Right now, you, as a part of the Millennial generation, are still living in a world primarily dominated by the ones before you. But soon, you will be the leaders. I believe wholeheartedly that you will be a generation that will change everything. You will change the face of politics and economics and commerce and technology. You are already heralding in the necessary changes that are over-due, even though you are still young, but soon you will truly make your mark.

And so, whether you are a Millennial or a seasoned mer-chant, I hope the dogmatic principles outlined in this book will speak to you, because there are certain fundamentals that you will need to remember moving forward that are timeless and generation-less and that I hope do not get lost in the revolution that you are poised to initiate.

# CHAPTER
# ONE

. . . . . . . . . . . . . . . . . . . . . . . . . . . . . .

# OUT OF STEP

. . . . . . . . . . . . . . . . . . . . . . . . . . . . . .

## WHEN CUSTOMER
## SERVICE GOES WRONG

I have no doubt that at one point (or many points) in your life, you have had a negative or unfavorable encounter with someone who was providing you with goods or services. In this chapter, I would like to explore examples of these types of interactions in order to introduce the basics of what to do and what not to do when engaging with your customers.

There are so many things that can go wrong in customer service, and you need to be aware of what could happen so that you can, hopefully, prevent it when dealing with your own customers. You must, as a shopkeeper or as an employee, be prepared because problems are inevitable. In order to prepare, you have to be able to recognize issues and mistakes that people can make. Just by being aware of wrongdoings, you are already on your way to preventing them. When learning something new, it is important to not only understand what to do but also to understand what *not* to do. This concept applies to customer service all the same.

This chapter outlines both glaring and subtle examples of poor customer service and unpacks why these instances happened as well as how to fix them. We will study examples of wrongdoings of specific companies, because if it can happen to those companies, it can happen to yours.

I have often been asked what my worst customer service experience was. Quite frankly, it is a story I like to tell. It was an incident that I personally had while flying with a small airline out of my home city. Prior to this airline coming onto the scene, passengers were still being plagued with certain issues with larger airlines. I was a frequent flier for business purposes, so I was intimately aware of the issues with one in particular. For many reasons, they had to cut back on a lot of staff. Thusly, because they were grossly understaffed, they didn't have enough manpower to properly deal with customers, leaving the customers themselves burdened. It was nearly impossible to receive proper service, even when things weren't hectic. Imagine how bad the service was when problems or delays did arise? It became a serious, serious issue and was only compounded over time.

I want to be clear, though, that it wasn't necessarily the fault of the employees. They were overloaded with work, stressed out about the stability of their jobs, and irritated about the lack of support from above. They were essentially left out to deal with customers at their own peril. The animosity employees felt for their employer was palpable, and the customers felt their indifference for their jobs. More often than not, when I asked for any assistance, I was told by an employee that what I had asked for "wasn't their job," Worse still, usually no referral came directing me to the one whose job it really was. If there even was such a person.

Prices rose and the planes were unkempt. It was a mess. When the loyal busy travellers, who had spent a considerable amount of money on premium business class tickets, booked a ticket using their accumulated points, the airlines treated what was essentially their best customers by giving them the broken seat (there always is one) and the last opportunity to choose a meal, even if they were sitting in the middle (there was guaranteed to only be one choice left—the one no one ever wanted). Time for a big change.

Then this lovely fresh new air service came along. They implemented a clear plan to right the wrongs of air travel in a big way—namely, in the customer service arena. Even their name signified their mission and their promise. Most often they can be found wearing a jaunty hat, a tailored uniform, and a big smile. Adamant about and projecting their desire to care for the customer, they treated us all the same, which is an important concept that will be discussed later. There were smaller, neater planes with leather seats, free snacks and drinks for everyone, and much more welcomed space. Their website was simple to use, and the design was inviting. They implemented a point system where you could pay in points and/or cash whenever you booked that was far easier and more flexible than previous systems—no waiting period. Their image made you feel very cared for. What a marvelous job all those people behind the scenes did to bring in the business.

I began to travel frequently with them. There were cracks in the veneer, but all in all, it was a pleasant experience. That is, until one particular flight in which I had booked a premium seat in the front row. With this particular seat, I was allowed priority boarding, and so I was the first one aboard the plane. When I got to my seat, there was a young man in an airline attendant's uniform sitting in my seat looking at paperwork. Where he wasn't was at the open door greeting people.

I pointed and politely told him that he was in my seat. I received no response from him. Again, I said "Oh, that's my seat."

The young man looked up at me and actually said, "Okay, I'll be done in a minute," and then looked back down at his papers.

There were passengers coming in behind me, and I wasn't sure what to do, so I then said, "I'm sure I need to take my assigned seat."

The flight attendant then snapped at me that he was "getting up," He stood up in a huff, threw his papers and pen back down onto "my" seat, and moved past me to the door of the plane where he should have already been stationed. The people behind me had started to push, and so I picked up his paperwork and put it on the seat next to mine in order to take my seat. The flight attendant watched me do this and then actually rudely advised me that he "was going to move it." He said this in front of the whole line. He was clearly very annoyed, and his voice was dripping with sarcasm and disdain. I couldn't imagine what the real problem was, but regardless of the reason, he never should have spoken to a customer in that tone.

Naturally, I had now become very irritated, and so I told him, "I have to take my seat, so I'm going to sit here. You knew that this was my seat and still you put your things here, so all I did was move your papers."

He just glared at me and then retorted, "Are we still talking about this?"

The airline lost me right then and there. From just one

person...from just one interaction. The worst part for me was that forty other people that were walking onto the plane had seen the negative interaction. My tense exchange with the flight attendant was the very first thing they had been greeted with as they boarded. What were *they* thinking? Was I an unruly passenger? Were there going to be delays or issues because of me?

I was embarrassed and hurt, but I didn't say a word as we lifted off and reached cruising altitude. I needed to get the situation, and flight, over with. But it didn't end, as the flight attendant came by with the food and beverage cart. He had had every opportunity to right his wrongs, and at this point should've apologized and moved forward, but he didn't. He could have saved himself graciously by telling me, "You know what, I'm so sorry. I wasn't supposed to be on this flight, but they threw me on here last minute, so I was rushing with paperwork. But it was the wrong paperwork..." Instead, he didn't smile, didn't look me in the eye, and didn't turn to me as he idled next to my seat with his food cart. I waved off a "No thank you," and he moved on, but not before I heard him ask the other customers if they would like anything to drink in a cheerful and upbeat tone.

As I sat in my seat, I realized that I was being punished for being a customer: he made me feel like I was the problem, and so the airline lost my support. It was sad, really, because they were such a great company to work through, with an expansive support network all geared toward a fantastic experience. And it all boiled down to one interaction—the one which is not at the very end of the line but the front line, the most important. And, honestly, they deserved to lose me.

Later that year, in that same airport where I was flying with a different airline, I came across that very same flight attendant. I could hear him from a mile away. He was very loud, very obnoxious, and very rude. The worst thing, though, was that he was wearing his airline's uniform. He was not only making himself look bad, but he was also making his company look bad. All I could do, as I watched him, was wonder what went wrong in the hiring and training process that they could have ended up with someone like him, for clearly mine wasn't just an isolated incident.

Now when I recall my experience with that airline, I don't think of the good things; all I can do is focus on this one indiscretion. It only takes one time to lose a customer.

There are ways and means that could have prevented this type of interaction from happening. They could retroactively turn it around, but they could have also been proactive about it. Simply put, they could have implemented better quality control checks on their employees. Likewise, co-workers must have an outlet to effectively share this information without being compromised themselves. I decided not to trust the other attendant by complaining and to just forget the situation and move on. They should be sending people out onto the floor and into the action to check on their staff. They should be sending agents out regularly, incognito, to gather performance information. Perhaps they do; perhaps this slipped through the cracks. By being proactive, you can rest assured your customers won't have to deal with incidences like the one I had.

No company should simply believe that if something happens, their customers will let them know on their own. That isn't always the case. Therefore, they should make sure to always give their customers ample opportunity to offer feedback. I never informed anyone about the incident, although I should have. Most customers won't complain; they will just walk away and never come back. And in the case of air travel, well, the best thing about it is when you have arrived at your destination and you're on your way to the rest of your day.

Many companies have adopted the system of sending surveys out through mail or email. These are helpful, but only sometimes. Most people don't open the surveys, or move them into their trash on their email. It doesn't seem like a lot to ask, but in reality, most customers don't believe they have the time to fill them out, and it's something that doesn't concern them *at the moment*. Now, there are certainly exceptions, with the most visible being Uber. Their system makes it easy to give feedback because all you have to do is choose one out of five stars on the payment page. Uber relieves the customer of stress because Uber eliminates options. Which eliminates taking too much time. You can choose one, two, three, four, or five stars. That's it. I've found that making communication easy for your customers is the fastest way to hear about their issues/worries/wishes.

In the vein of the airline story, I want to discuss a totally contrasting experience that I have had at the Toronto International Airport. Pearson is very large and handles more than seventy-five passenger airlines. I want to make it clear that this is not a boutique, but a rather large, factory-like airport that one would find in any large city. For flights to the United States, we must go through customs and immigration at our end first, which sometimes is an easy process; however, most of the time it's a hectic busy one. In order to help take care of their customers, Toronto Airport has put specific people in place after the customs counters whose sole job it is to offer help. Stationed at the beginning of the line where you drop your luggage and at the end of the line where you are screened are two amazing people who make this an actually enjoyable experience. They are positioned at the most stressful points time-wise and are there to keep order, and to mediate any potential issues. But it is all about how they do it.

Picture this: various stressed, delayed or tired customers, nervous that they could potentially miss their flights, enter the security area. We are promptly greeted by a jolly man in a porter's uniform who kindly asks them for their bags. He is always quick to take the children's and women's first. This lovely man then loads the bags onto a conveyor belt for us, which is essentially our job, all the while singing and whistling a merry tune. A woman, the greeter, stands at the other end of the queue. She manages the people in line, at the point where stress is directly related to time. She keeps people moving. If anyone is running late, all they have to do is let her know, and she will move them appropriately. She is able to address all of the customers at once, but still makes you feel as though she is addressing you personally. In a loud, happy voice, she reassures us all that the best part of our day is about to happen, we will make our flights, we are going on vacation!

She is able to put a smile on my face every time. When I step ahead through the priority line, she almost always lets the others now held back know that she simply must let the pretty lady through. That's something she doesn't have to do—the signs are clear. Jokingly, she scolds businessmen to get off their phones, or little kids to throw away water bottles, but she does it in a way that endears herself to them.

These two people, the porter and the greeter, alone are worth their weight in gold. Upon entering their domain, you can visibly see shoulders relax, most smile, and some even laugh! It's hard not to: the porter is so charming in the way that he sings. The only blues in that part of the airport are the ones that he croons!

This is an example of a perfect execution of the dance of customer service. When customer service really works, and when customers can rely on consistent, quality service, they relax; they trust. In turn, customers are more open, friendly, and helpful to the people servicing them.

But when customer service goes bad, when the dance falls apart, the consequences are dire because you run the great possibility of losing a customer for good.

The really important thing to understand is that even though, like in the case with the relatively new airline, it took only one employee to ruin their reputation with me, that employee does not stand alone. He is part of a greater system. If one crucial piece is flawed, it may mean the whole system is flawed. Yes, it is sometimes the case that the employee just should not interact with customers, but that is a rare case. More often, that employee fails the business because the business has failed the employee. There are numerous points where this can happen.

Perhaps the hiring process is broke. In this instance, the shopkeeper needs to map out what he wants out of a customer service agent, and then he should be able to identify the correct person. Problems don't always come out until employees start working, but there are methods in which to find out if you simply have hired the wrong person for the job. More often than not, if you're the shopkeeper, then you've most likely been through the ranks, and so you have experience and can judge that for yourself. Keep yourself available to new hires and always be aware of what they are doing. We all have bad days, and if you aren't watching enough, you might only stumble upon a bad day for an otherwise great employee. Perhaps the employee that you are having issues with just does not fit well with the dynamic of the other employees. In that case, it is important to try different things, put different people together—different ages, different styles, different genders, or different personalities. Sometime you'll be surprised by the dance you can create if you just switch up partners.

It is also possible that the training that the business offers the employee is insufficient. It is important to make sure that your employees have all of the tools necessary for them to do the job. If they don't have them, then it is your responsibility to offer them.

It is equally possible that your managers have improperly managed your employees. Improper management results in an inadequate support system for employees, which in turn results in inadequate employees.

Lastly, it is possible that you, as a shopkeeper, have not fulfilled your obligation, and that is why your employees are inadequate. Perhaps you haven't properly outlined their duties, explained your objectives, or you haven't acquired enough of them. You must make sure that your staff can understand your business philosophy, your product, and your ultimate goal. It is so important to realize that this dance between customer service representatives and the customer is made possible because of the shopkeeper. Therefore, you must maintain a vigilant eye for any missteps and quickly, and efficiently, fix them.

It is clear to the customer when this dance is done well. When you walk into an experience that has unforgettable customer service, you can just feel it. You can see that everyone has a specific position, has been trained properly, and knows what they must do. You can also tell that everyone is comfortable enough in their jobs so that when problems arise, they can fix them professionally. When the dance is just right, you know because employees feel empowered that they have a purpose and feel that they are an important function of a business. The rules apply to everyone, so you need to be an example!

If you have tried everything to fix a problematic employee who is just not doing the job as it's been explained, you have to be prepared to be able to deal with that. As much as your customer service rep cannot ignore the customer's needs and look away and must deal with a problem, you have to do the same. It's the shopkeeper's issue if somebody has to go. When that happens, you must be prepared. You cannot be afraid to fire someone. I know people in business who can't do the firing. They can do the hiring, but they don't have it in them to fire someone. You need to understand that's a very important point—a critical point in providing good customer service.

I talk so much about the importance of customer service because customer service is always about making a sale. Nothing can happen with your business unless you can get the customer to that purchasing point. This purchasing point is the starting point for the success of your business.

The sale is not solely reliant upon your brilliant idea, nor your novel product, nor your impressive co-founder, nor your great work ethic, nor your expensive marketing plan. It is dependent upon the moment when that customer walks into your world and steps up to the register. So if your operation is not pointed toward the care of your customer, then you have mismanaged your resources. Because it's all about making your promise to the customer and delivering on it.

For example, I had the wonderful opportunity to work with a delightful woman who had a dream to open a little café in her small home town. She is a very caring, inviting woman who loves to bake, and, after many years working for the government, she desired to take the leap into capitalizing on those skills and be her own boss. So we worked together to build it. I function primarily as support and management, and I help to develop recipes and menus, as well as the concept design. I do not need to be physically there all the time; we work well together, and the bakery runs very smoothly.

This is mostly due to the fact that, when training and hiring, we make sure to engrain within our employees the idea that taking care of the customer comes first. As an employee, you should always remember that customers do not care that you are tired because your upstairs neighbour threw a dance party until 4:00 a.m. They do not care that you were late opening the café because your cat got sick all over your living room. They don't care that your shirt was unwashed because you forgot to go to the Laundromat for a third day in a row. They don't care about the *whys*. They just care about the fact that you are tired and grumpy, or late to get them their morning coffee, or look unprofessional and unkempt. They just want to have an epic purchase experience (literally) and get on with their day.

There are no excuses. You are only in this for the customers' moment, and if you try to blather about things unless asked (and even then keep it short), customers will not listen. They don't want to hear you talk. All they want is to watch you run, not walk, to the machine and make them that cappuccino as fast as you can. Mostly.

It is important for the employees to bustle, to hear all about the "Customer's" day/issues/concerns (that's right, capital C) and let them know that their "day just got better." But, most importantly, the staff must know this: If you're talking, you're not listening! By listening, you are able to care for the customer by understanding exactly what he or she wants.

We made our promise. Our customers will enjoy great

baked goods, better coffee, and made-daily wholesome food, so we will follow through. If the latte isn't frothy enough, we will make you a new one. If the salad or the biscuits aren't fresh enough, we will fix that. Fortunately, that rarely happens, as we have set our standards and expectations and have trained well. We also take ownership when problems arise. We don't break our promise to the customer! Don't let catty co-workers, double shifts, or late nights prevent you from delivering the promise you made.

It's a simple formula. When we deliver on that promise-with well-trained, gracious staff and a great product, we have happy customers. When we have happy customers, we have committed customers. When we have committed customers, they open their wallets and our business grows. The café grows so rapidly, the owner can barely keep up.

It truly is a sight to see when walking into her café. Customers are relaxed, happy, smiling, and laughing. We are often the best moment in their day. When they are happy, my staff is happy. And they gain confidence because they can tell that they have succeeded in their work. Therefore, they are empowered to make decisions themselves. This is a very important place for any employee to be.

In contrast, the flight attendant on that fateful flight failed to keep the promise of his airline. He did not uphold their promise that I would be treated better with them. This failing of customer service in Canada was the norm for a really long time.

It is my opinion that customer service declined in Canada in the '80s and early '90s due to a rapidly growing and changing workplace environment. Gone were the owner/operators of the '50s and '60s. No longer did the gas station owners stand outside in a crisp grey uniform to greet you and gas up your car with a very polite smile. The new generation, my generation, transformed that picture. Not only were our ideals different from those of our parent's generation, but we were also having to deal with a rapidly growing technology sector. The workplace was becoming more automated: phones and computers replaced human-to-human contact. The world of business was becoming a twenty-four-hour day, and the speed at which things happened doubled, tripled, and even quadrupled! And during all this, we didn't seem to adapt customer service to our new era; we seem to have just left it behind.

The importance of customer service just simply wasn't attached to our new business model.

Today, I believe that we have come full circle. We have

figured out how to use technology to bring back outstanding customer service, albeit, in a very different way than before. Our laptops and cell phones have provided us with the ability to have instantaneous access to our business, our products, our services, our employees, and our customers twenty-four hours a day. Today, customers demand phenomenal customer service, and because competition is so fierce, companies must oblige.

So when expectations run so high, shopkeepers must be aware of the mistakes that result in poor customer service. The number-one mistake that shopkeepers make is that they believe all their employees think like them. It might be frustrating to the shopkeeper that not all his or her employees have the same vision, knowledge or understanding. But look at it this way. There is a reason why a beehive has one queen and tens of thousands of worker bees. What would happen if all of the bees were queen bees and they all knew better than each other? There would be a systemic breakdown. The workers know their jobs and do their jobs very well. The queen bee knows her job and is always present and making sure that everything happens accordingly. As a shopkeeper, you want your employees to know the business procedures that you worked hard to put in place, and you want them to honour those procedures. More importantly, though, you should never assume that your employees are on the same wavelength or have the same thought process as you do and therefore neglect to help them learn the dance. Your role is to teach, to impress upon them, to watch, and to be open to continually learning or adapting yourself depending on what challenges you ultimately face.

The second common mistake that shopkeepers make with their employees is issuing poor or inadequate training. Sometimes it is the case where no training is given because of time or money constraints. Training should be administered at all costs. This cost usually comes in the form of your own blood, sweat, and tears. If you reach deep down inside yourself, you'll be amazed what you find there. The reward is tremendous. Training should never be too short; it should be written in plain language in a manual or guide and continually updated, and progress should be documented. Your staff is an asset as much as your product is an asset—care for them accordingly.

A third mistake is not allowing your customer service staff to feel empowered. By allowing them to feel empowered to make some decisions in their interactions with customers, or when situations arise, you allow them to learn through trial and error. I've seen situations where bosses don't trust their employees, or don't empower them, and then get angry when something happens and their employees are too afraid to take charge. Situations arise all of the time, and sometimes the shopkeeper is unavailable to help. Therefore, we must allow the employee to try. Start small and let it grow. If it works, great! If it doesn't (be available to know it didn't), then I work with my employees to figure out what should change. This is a practice that we are always partaking in with the café employees. At the end of the day, we talk about the issues or situations encountered during that day. The conversations usually flow as follows:

ME: "OK, so what happened out there today?"

EMPLOYEE: "A, B, C happened."

ME: "Was every customer happy today?"

EMPLOYEE: "Yes, except for one."

ME: "What happened?"

EMPLOYEE: "We were swamped, and by the time she got her coffee, it was cold."

ME: "What did you do about that?"

At this point, I would expect an employee who did not feel empowered to have reacted to the situation by apologizing and continuing on to the next customer. But my employees at the café are trained well enough that they know that they can take charge of a situation. And the conversation would continue as follows:

EMPLOYEE: "Well, I apologized to her with a smile, took her cold coffee, ran back to the machine, made her a fresh one, and returned it. I also told her that both coffees were on the house."

ME: "That was the right thing to do! Thank you. Did you happen to deal with any other customer during this interaction?"

EMPLOYEE: "No, I took care of it right away."

ME: "Excellent. You showed your commitment for everyone else to see, not just the unhappy customer. You made sure to focus on her so that she knew you had the power to fix her situation immediately."

This type of conversation is exceedingly important to have with your employees. It shows that you can trust them, and it makes your staff feel that much more important. You want to give your staff the ability to feel important, because if you value their opinions and you ask them for their thoughts and feelings, etc., it makes them feel a sense of ownership of the business. When they feel this ownership, they will care.

If the employee, in the case of the cold coffee, had made the wrong decision, I would not admonish her for it! I would simply talk with her about the appropriate response, and I can guarantee that next time, the situation will unfold differently. That is the point behind our regular discussions.

Thinking short term is another mistake to avoid. In most cases, businesses aren't profitable in the short term. The beginning is often rocky. It takes time and patience before you get that winning combination of staff and product. As a shopkeeper, you must work hard before things start to click for you, and so you must be very flexible in the beginning. You must be willing to change things up with your staff regularly to see what works the best. You must continue to train, evaluate, hire, and fire before the dance becomes fluid. It will take quite a lot of practice and many dances in order to get it just right.

Sometimes, the shopkeeper makes the mistake of simply hiring the wrong individual; the tone-deaf person who just can't dance with the team. When you hire the wrong person for your team, it brings down the whole team. I don't care what that employee's last name is or who he/she is sleeping with. Don't hire your friend's cousin's daughter if she is wrong for the job! Nor your sister-in-law! Nor your boyfriend! If that employee is wrong for the job, not only will you and your team suffer, but that employee will suffer as well. He will know that he is ill-suited and that there may be little he can do to change that fact. He might become indifferent to the work at hand, and if you want to get ahead of your competition, your employees cannot be indifferent. When this happens, the employee does not care for your customer. He simply wants to get in and get out. An example would be a situation where a customer walks in five minutes before closing time and asks if he can still make a purchase. An indifferent employee would not be able to hide that he wants the man to take a hike. "We're closing" is all he offers. An employee who is not indifferent sees the potential final sale, knows he is *not* closed yet, and would say something like, "Absolutely. What can I help you with? This part of the kitchen is closed up, but I can surely get something out of the fridge for you."

The first is an example of an employee putting himself before the customer. These types of situations happen all of the time, and each time your employee has the ability to make a choice. You don't have to pray that she makes the right one; you can make sure of that by hiring the right person. You don't have to hope; you can put yourself in a situation where you know.

Lastly, it is important for your customer service reps, or anyone who is interacting with your customers, to be happy. They have to be happy. If you, as a shopkeeper, are not providing them with a nice, clean, comfortable, fair workspace and work environment, they will not be happy.

Keep customer service representatives happy by being visible, being approachable, and being available so they can talk to you. It is also important to reward them. You can do it through raises at appropriate times, but you can also take them to lunch, congratulate them on wins, or simply find your voice and let them know that you appreciate them.

You can also keep them happy by being happy yourself. Of course, running or owning a business is an incredibly stressful job, but your staff feeds off of your energy. Do not be gruff or short; do not treat them like they are dumb, or get irritated when they ask (what you think is) a stupid question. If you are impatient, or rude, or don't have time for them, that behaviour will translate to the customer.

If your employees are happy and comfortable in their work environment, this shows the customer that the shopkeeper cares about them, which is something that will go a long way with them.

This leads me to a discussion about why employees can still fail you in regard to customer service even when all of the previously discussed points are met. Service staff can still fail because they believe that offering good customer service takes too long. Employees also might suffer from inherent complacency, and others might become blasé over time.

It is amazing how much time it takes to properly train and continue to train your employees. A lot of people will skip that necessary time, but this time is important for both the shopkeeper and the employee. They both must be present in order to train together and should continue to make time to practice together after official training ends. If the shopkeeper is heavily involved in this process, she will be able to tell when the employee is ready, where the employee's weak points are, and what he really excels at.

You absolutely need to practice, practice, practice! During this time, you are teaching your employee aspects of the dance. You must make sure to teach him specific steps in the dance such as where his station is, what each aspect of his job requires, and how he should handle specific situations. Since you, the shopkeeper, are giving him all of this initial direction, there will be no question about what your preferred methods are. The preferred methods are what *you* dictate, and so best practices will be uniform across your whole team.

After training, you must allow your staff to practice. For this practice, it is crucial that you are present. Don't leave your staff alone on that dance floor! Watch them operate in the workplace. See how they interact with customers and their co-workers. During this time, lend them a hand; be there at all times to answer any questions they may have. You can't throw them to the lions until you are assured that they are comfortable. Let's face it; you can't see them move until you can get them on the floor. But be on that dance floor with them. All shopkeepers may have different methods of training, but this final step should be standard. You don't have to know everything upfront, so rest assured that there is always flexibility to tweak your employees after the fact.

Complacency is another barrier employers must overcome in order to offer great customer service. This speaks to cultural or societal norms, more often than not. In Canada, there was a general feeling that you would "always have a job." It is changing now, but this type of thinking is still prevalent in our national thought. The thing with complacency is that it engenders a sort of attitude that is really detrimental to the dance of customer service. It makes some believe that, probably, they don't have to give it their all out on that dance floor. They don't care to become a better performer.

Blasé employees are another issue. This type of attitude was so prevalent in Canada in the past (think 1995–2010) it was even parodied on comedy shows. We are, fortunately, seeing more and more today those who are truly talented in service and are in the right job for them. We are definitely putting more demands on it and speaking out about it.

Now, though, the culture is generally changing towards the more of customer service. This is primarily because of the emergence of new competition, and not because it's local. The Internet and ease of purchase through it has ensured that.

Frankly, it was the Canadian shopkeepers who were allowing this type of blasé or complacent behaviour to run amok in their businesses. It took competition for us to change the service culture, which is reality. There was an inundation of chain stores in the power cities in Canada, and slowly, these companies seeped into the smaller towns. I have been a small business owner myself, and I understand the plight of the person who works hard to keep his own business, especially with the task of finding and working with something to offer that's special or unique. Or a service that is simply done very well and that a reputation can be built upon. Unfortunately, though, the older generations, for the most part, still buy based on price and so welcomed the shoe stores, bookstores, print centres, etc., into towns without even knowing where their dollar eventually ended up. Fortunately, Millennials understand that value supersedes price, and we may see trends reverse. And by value I don't just mean the product or service; it refers as well to supporting both home and local business.

When these chains arrive, you know about them simply by their reputation. You know exactly what type of products and service you will receive before you even walk through their door. This is because chain stores are identical to each other: if you've been to one, you've been to them all. They take the time and energy away from the consumer of having to worry what they are going to get. It remains consistent. The products are the same and the employees are the same. These companies rely on their reputation, and in most cases, you are there for the name brand, not the experience.

Starbucks is a perfect example of this. Go to any Starbucks and watch the people in line. Most of them don't care where they are or how they are being treated. Heck, most of them never even look up from their cell phones! The great irony in that is that those people have, in their hands, the best resource ever invented (so far) in order to find a great coffee shop that offers possibly cheaper and possibly better coffee and great customer service right around the block! But they don't care, because they are at Starbucks. The product may or may not be great, and it likely isn't noticed how hard the employees are working, because the brand name has already made that sale. And so we must step up. There is no room for slouching. Grabbing your customers' attention is one thing, but be prepared to dazzle them with your service.

Quite some time ago now, deep within a large corporation, there was another great example of how the lack of competition in Canada engendered a lacking customer service culture. There was an inherent structural weakness within the company itself, but customers didn't have a choice but to continue to use them. In turn, the company was never wanting for customers. Because they were never desperate for customers, they simply continued business as usual and were never forced to appropriately address their shortcomings. The key word being forced. As in a timely manner, or simply identifying and facing the real problem no matter where it lie, top, middle, or bottom. The right attention was not where it should have been— that is, on the ones making the purchase. Resources did not appear to be placed efficiently or correctly.

It got so bad at one point, after cutting back so severely, the front line staff we were left dealing with were disgruntled and dismantled. They just couldn't be nice. They hated the position they were in because they were overworked and/or not supported and, so of course they directed their frustration towards us. What's more, their behaviour led us to believe that the situation was not being addressed. When the only person you have available to you says things like "that's not my job" and leaves it at that without showing you who you should address your issues/needs/requests to, while it is very clear there is no other visible outlet, then *Houston we have a problem.*

The times were rife with a joke among business circles that I think says everything anyone needs to know. The joke goes roughly like this: There is a guy in a bar having a drink. He notices a lovely woman enter in clothing indicative of her industry. He asks her who she works for, but she won't acknowledge him. So, what he does is he starts to sing out the different jingles from in and around the industry to see if he can get her to smile.

Finally, the woman snaps at him. "What on earth do you want?!"

He snaps his fingers and points to her. "Got it," he says, and aptly names the company.

Inevitably, with increasing competition, they were forced

to change, and so were their ridiculous prices. But still, I feel the legacy will be hard for them to get completely out from under. On the other hand, they were right to keep going, keep working, and keep adapting and focusing on improvement. It is very evident today that enough changed within to provide far better service. That being said, however, the only direction they could go was up.

Although interacting with the employees was difficult and grating, I blame the higher-ups. We believed the company as a whole was mismanaged and if anyone had taken the time to identify and admit to this, then maybe the reputation could have been saved.

You need to remember the fundamentals of management: observe, analyze, and be conscious of what is going on.

**OBSERVE:**

They could have observed the interactions between their employees and their customers both in person and online. Managers must, first, be able to observe. If you are a manager, ask yourself a couple of questions. *Are you there walking the floor? Are your offices separate from where your employees are located or are you situated among them? Are your employees spread out where you can't monitor them very well? Are you available to your employees? Are you setting aside time throughout your day to spend time with them?*

**ANALYZE:**

Once you can gather the raw data from observing, analyze it. During this process, don't be afraid to go back to the basics. Think: *Are your employees keeping the promise to your customers and delivering it?* Make sure to interpret this data in order to make changes. This job is almost always too big for just the shopkeeper to do. You must put systems in place for this. Spread this job out to all departments—to all managers—in order to get a big picture assessment. Tap people and ask them to assist you. If the data you are getting back doesn't add up, if the movement is off, then something is broken "somewhere," Perhaps the company in the previous story could have used more service agents at counters (they could have). Perhaps they could have given their agents the wherewithal to make decisions and take action (they could have). Perhaps they could have had faster response times over email (they could have). Perhaps they could have let the public know they were aware of the situation and would be addressing it (they should have). As a shopkeeper analyze your observations in order to understand what went badly, what went well, and what was just okay.

**BE CONSCIOUS:**

Lastly, be conscious of what is going on. This is a crucial function of the shopkeeper. If you can't be conscious of your business, then you need to re-evaluate your position.

By that I mean, you need to remember that even if your business is a friendly local lawn cutting service, or you are an independent film producer, it is still a business. There is still a bottom line that you need to get to. No matter what happens, there will always be a bottom line. There is a great scene in Russell Crowe's *Cinderella Man* that speaks to this point. Russell Crowe's character addresses his manager and asks him to be compassionate with him. But, the manager can't. He tells him that his heart is for his family, but his brain and his balls are for business... and this is business.

Let's apply this process to a real-life scenario:

There is a small muffin store run by a woman who charges seven dollars for one muffin. This price sounds ludicrous but, take it from me they are absolutely worth it. They are also nutritional and specialized. In addition, the shop is well laid out and inviting. It's a small store; there is only a takeout counter and a small kitchen in the back. One day, I went to grab a muffin and, as I was waiting in line, I noticed that one of the employees was sitting off to the side of the checkout, taking a break while still wearing her apron. She had her phone out and was doing her best to not make eye contact with any customer in line. Meanwhile, her co-worker was unable to keep up with the line at the counter, and customers (who were willing to pay seven dollars for a single muffin!) were actually leaving the line and walking out. While I observed the employee who was on her phone, I saw that there were very important, inherent, issues and that the business was suffering because of it. You cannot afford to lose customers if you want to sell a muffin for seven dollars!

I knew that the woman who owned the bakeshop probably had been up at 5:00 a.m. to bake the muffins and, because it was late afternoon, had left to go home. All I could think of was that this woman wasn't there in order to *observe* this incident, but, hopefully, she would hear about it later and work to *analyze* it and take steps to prevent the problem.

If it were me, and I was the shopkeeper, I would analyze this situation and then sit down with that particular employee. In the blank spaces provided, please write down the three things that you think I would tell the employee regarding the rules that she broke. You can compare your answers to mine, which are outlined in the following paragraph.

1. _____

2. _____

3. _____

I would tell her that since she worked in a fast-paced, food service environment, when she wasn't working to service the customer, she needed to be out of the way and certainly not in uniform. I would also tell her that if she needed to be on her phone while on break, she again must set herself away from the waiting customer. When she is looking down at her phone and not making eye contact with anyone who is tied up in the line (they just may know she is an employee), nothing is more annoying. Lastly, and most importantly, I would tell her that if she wanted to use her phone during break, she *must*, absolutely *must*, wash her hands after! I can only imagine where it has been. I know where they go! PSA: Put the phone away, and for the love of God, don't stick it in your back pocket! When I see one on a wait staff, I have to wonder, why is it there? Is that person picking it up for personal use while on duty? But I also need to rely on the other staff members to relate the observation to me in a timely manner. Can I? Have the means for that been set up?

If that girl had been a better employee, she might have been more conscious of her co-worker being swamped and would have run to wash her hands and then jumped in to help her, even if she was on break—if only for a moment.

Let's analyze another real-world story about poor customer service when face-to-face:

This example comes from an experience I had with a woman who was working reception at a car dealership. The woman had one of those pasted-on smiles that kind of make me cringe. They also put me off on the wrong foot right away because I always feel as though they are looking straight through me. As I approached her desk, I could almost see the gears working behind her veneer; she was sizing me up to determine if I was going to be a sale or not. That was highly inappropriate; sales come in all shapes and sizes, don't they? I could see her decide on her own that I was not going to be one (silly her, for I laugh inside at people who do that when they have no idea who they are dealing with) and my suspicion was confirmed when I got up to her counter and said, "Hi, I'm Shari, my son dropped my car off to have it serviced."

She stared. I told her my name again, and she proceeded to address me as a Mrs. and as Shirley. Wrong on both accounts. She asked me what it was I needed, and again, I told her that I needed to check on my service. She seemed to not process what I was saying. When it finally registered, she just pointed to somewhere "over there." She didn't apologize or give me any other information. At this point, sales staff were walking over to greet me. However, as soon as they heard "service," they turned and walked away.

Finally, after much confusion, and with prodding from a second person, I was sent over to a customer service rep, who was lovely. Unfortunately for that rep, I was already irritated and regardless of her cheery demeanour, my opinion about the establishment was already set.

When it comes to these face-to-face interactions, consistency across the floor is important.

In the blank space, *analyze* the five mistakes that were made in that last story. You can refer to the following paragraph for answers and explanations.

1. _____

2. _____

3. _____

4. _____

5. _____

First, the receptionist didn't listen to what I needed. She assumed that I needed sales, when I really needed service. After I told her what I needed, she was visibly disappointed in my answer. Second, the layout of the business should be altered so that people in need of service do not have to walk through the sales floor, although their reason for this should not escape you. By having people that only need service walk through the sales floor, the company has created an awkward situation. At the very least, make it clear then where I can direct myself. It does not feel good to be warmly approached by sales associates only to be ignored the second that they realize they can't make commission off of you. Third, the receptionist used the wrong name. I hate being called Shirley. I'm not Shirley! If she hadn't heard my name, there would have been absolutely no harm in asking me to repeat myself. I don't even mind if she had asked me much later on in the conversation and not right away. That would have showed me that she cared. Fourth, she called me "Mrs." which was not the way I addressed myself in our exchange. Do not assume. When in doubt, it is common courtesy to use "Ms." Lastly, it was unnecessary for two people to need to consult with me before they could figure out to whom I needed to speak. When a team is inefficient when trying to accomplish a simple task, it speaks volumes to me about the business as a whole.

Now let's analyze an incident that occurred during an over-the-phone interaction:

It is also important to discuss customer service errors

that can occur over the phone. Good online or telephonic customer service is a little trickier to accomplish simply because some of the "human" element is gone. It is easier to feel like you can get away with being a jerk over the phone because of the anonymity factor. Don't take your online or telephonic customer service for granted just because of this! It is extremely important to talk about mistakes that can happen in this medium.

Here is a story that speaks to mistakes that happen over telephonic communication. I was a member of a specialized health training center for which I paid an automatic monthly fee. Over time, I found that I wasn't really utilizing all that this company had to offer, and I had found a smaller one that fit my needs much better. I wanted to try out the other company for a longer period, so I decided to take advantage of my training center's offer that I could suspend my membership for a month or two without the fees. My children, who were also on the membership plan, also felt as though they were not necessarily getting everything out of it, so I wanted to find out if it was even worth continuing. I needed help, so I called in to the training center, and the receptionist answered. She rarely answered the phones when they rang, so I was surprised that she had answered in the first place. I told her my name and that I wanted to put my membership on hold. I told her that I was going out of town, and so I needed to take care of it that day before I left. I also explained to her that since I didn't know how the process worked, I would need to actually speak to someone who could help me. She was silent on the other end.

I asked her if she knew if anyone was available to help me. She wasn't sure. I actually did have cause to wonder at that point if she had even been listening to me. I could tell that she did not take any information down, so that led me to believe that she probably would not even remember my name after she hung up. Finally, after more prodding on my part, she told me that I should probably speak to someone named Gregory.

"Great!" I said, "Can you put him on the phone?" She told me that she couldn't do that, but that she could transfer me to his number. So, getting somewhere, I agreed.

She transferred me to Gregory, and I was dumped right into his voicemail. I left a very detailed message for him explaining everything I had questions about. But because I was leaving on business, I informed him that I really wanted to speak to a live person to get this taken care of or I might lose the time.

I called the receptionist back. She "hmmd" at me and forwarded me to the exact same number.

I didn't hear back from Gregory for two weeks. When he finally rang me, I knew immediately that he had me on speakerphone in his office. He simply said he received a message from me and asked what it was regarding, no mention of the details I had given. I could also hear him fiddling around with something in the background. I can always tell when someone is facing away from the speaker, so I knew that he wasn't entirely focusing his attention on me. It almost sounded like he had his feet up on the desk; I could just sense it from him. His first comment was defensive, as he tried to explain that he had been away sick. I didn't buy it for a second.

Very loudly I said jokingly, "Holy Cow, it's been so long since I left that message, about two weeks!" All of a sudden, I could hear him jump and shuffle to grab the phone. Was someone within earshot of this conversation or was it for *my* sake? I said, "Yes, take me off speaker. Now let's get down to business," in my boardroom voice. I could tell that he was suddenly sitting up straight. I then again explained what I wanted, but in a concise manner. He assured me that he could take care of it for me but there were options.

His position reversed, and suddenly, Gregory became the perfect person to speak to. He explained what I needed to know in clear words and helped me work through the options. He was very knowledgeable. During the conversation, I made sure to explain to him that the process was unclear and that I was unaware of the thirty-day notice that I needed to give them in order to use the hold. He apologized and gave me the hold immediately. He understood that they had made a mistake, and he was making an attempt to fix it. I appreciated his efforts but did explain to him that I was considering cancelling my membership, especially in light of the fact that every time I called the center, I was never properly serviced.

In the space that follows, brainstorm some of the missteps that occurred at the health center. Next, write a couple of sentences about what you think could have been done to save the situation or prevent something like it from happening again. You can find all of the answers in the subsequent paragraph.

Your Answer:

_____

_____

_____

_____

The issue started with the receptionist. We've established that she didn't listen to me, but the bigger mistake was that she did not have a logbook or notebook by her side to take down my message. How would she remember to follow-up? What would remind her to make sure to check back to be sure that Gregory indeed helped me out? She should have written down my name and had it spelled out, or repeated it so she could get it right. She also should have taken my phone number in order to make sure that someone could follow-up with me. Her employer should have provided her with this notebook. Next, the receptionist didn't even try to find someone in person to ask where she should send me. I've been in that establishment plenty of times. I know that there is always staff close by! Further, based on my call-in, she should have found someone for me to talk to; instead, she just sent me straight on to what was unknown. At the very least, perhaps she could have checked up with Gregory to make sure that he had gotten my message. If Gregory truly was sick, she should have known not to send me to his voicemail, or upon finding that out, she should have let someone else know there was an important issue to deal with that was likely left on his voicemail! Lastly, even this girl could have called me back to check in with me! No, she simply left me lost in cyberspace.

The final straw was the additional mistakes that Gregory

made: It took him two weeks to respond. He put me on speakerphone; he didn't apologize, and he presumably lied to me about being sick. His attitude was off as well. He wasn't on the offensive to try to win me back. Instead, he was defensive and short with me. He also didn't take the time to assess my issue before he called me back, despite the fact that I had left him a clear message about what I wanted from him. He should have called me with a plan of action at the ready. He appeared indifferent to me and to the possibility of losing me as a customer.

In the end, the real issue originated from the receptionist. She did not handle this correctly. But where does the problem lie? Perhaps she was stretched too thin, with no available support for all that she was responsible for, or she didn't have the tools to successfully accomplish it. Possibly she could have been filling in for someone and it was not her normal job, but she failed to be humble and graciously attempt to help nevertheless. She simply was not willing to do her job effectively and certainly not willing or capable of following up herself. Was it her training? Perhaps Gregory himself was stretched thin, or he truly was sick. A co-worker wasn't set up to cover for him? Maybe he himself is the shopkeeper who was complacent in his role and the success of the company. Maybe he forgot the importance of maintaining that which he had worked hard for. It's possible. He certainly had all the answers and the power to make important decisions. The real problem isn't always simple, or obvious.

Let's practice our analysis exercises with one last example:

I am a member of a different, very large, gym and athletic facility, which has approximately ten thousand active members. This gym offers a variety of services from regular cardio classes to workout rooms to a kids club. They also have racquetball courts, a swimming pool, personal training, nutritional counselling, a spa, a salon, and a café. They have it all!

The facility has to be very well staffed in order to ensure that everything runs smoothly. There are attendants placed directly in front of the guests as they enter the lobby. Their job is to check the guests in, provide guest passes, or refer guests to an account services member. They also answer calls and direct them to the appropriate person. Regardless of time of day, the two on the desk are always busy but, most importantly, they are always "on."

Any customer can clearly see that they are always on task, not just because of their upbeat attitudes, but because they wear an ear/microphone piece that is attached to a unit clipped at their waists. This piece links them directly to others in the building. All staff (including the managers) can hear all that is happening by being connected. This is key because they are all able to instantaneously communicate their needs to the appropriate person. A system has also been put in place to alert the staff via the use of a "code." All staff are clearly trained on this and exactly who is to immediately respond. For example, there is a code for guests trying to bypass the desk and get in without a valid pass or membership. There is a code for a lit signal that appears at the front desk indicating that an emergency button in the changing rooms or whirlpool has been pushed. There is a code for a new guest requesting to speak to an account representative, for a child who is missing, or for a guest who is causing an issue. All the front desk has to do is say the code (one word, a colour I believe) and immediately two staff members, appropriate to the issue, step up to address the situation. In the case of an emergency, they run to the site, prepared.

This system is incredibly impressive in its efficiency and effectiveness. But what is more important here besides the obvious? Use the word bank to fill in the blanks that follow. There will be leftover words at the end.

**WORD BANK:**

Safety, Speaking, Secretive, The Earpiece, Communication, Trained, Minimal Amount, Enough, Taught, Lying, Fairness, Catching

The key functioning element here for the staff is
_____, facilitating their roles.

Having effective _____ is an important aspect
of the front lobby.

The owners smartly placed _____ properly
_____ staff.

The code was set up to ensure both _____ and
_____ to the customer.

**ANSWERS:**

The Earpiece
Communication
Enough
Trained
Safety
Fairness

From this word bank, locate the *most critical word* in terms
of customer support for the centre and then place important related words around it. There will be some extra words.

**WORD BANK:**

Engagement, Discretion, Creativity, Reaction Time, Communication, Safety, Autonomy, Fairness, Professionalism

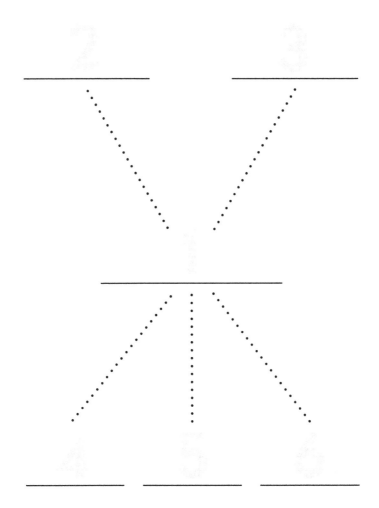

**ANSWERS:**

1. Communication
2. Discretion
3. Reaction Time
4. Professionalism
5. Fairness
6. Safety

Answers Explained:

This system is so great because it is set up with respect to safety and fairness to its members, which speaks, ultimately, to the promise that the facility made to them when they signed up. This promise of safety is acted out in a swift and exceedingly discreet and professional way so as not to cause unnecessary stress on the clients nor embarrassment to a particular member. There is no shouting or frenetic stir being generated (unless necessary of course) and the appropriate amount and required type of staff is always on hand. The communication system is set up properly between the necessary few who are on the front line and those who can take care of business. This, to me, is a most perfect example of the dance. But there is something further happening within the environment that I can see when looking closely, as I am so often doing. Something very, very important. The staff are not just smiling at the customers, they are smiling at each other. Attention given to pulling together a team that can work together with shared pride and respect for their jobs, each other, and their leaders has clearly been established. There is no (evident) animosity or all its other nasty relatives; rather, they appear to enjoy sharing the workplace and supporting each other in an honest way. Bravo.

It is so important for you to be able to analyze cases, and I hope that by working through them together, you can learn methods that you can apply in real-life situations. Let's discuss what methods you can take from this book to apply to your own business.

**Look, learn, and watch potential competition.** This applies to both the customer service people and to the shopkeeper. Ask yourself, "Who is successful? Why are they successful? What is happening at that business that is not happening at mine?" Here's a piece of great advice if you are able: be a customer. Go to your competition and be their customer. Investigate their strengths and weaknesses. Do they have enough staff? Is the service different from yours? Why are they outselling you? In the end, you don't need to copy their strategies, but just be aware of them.

**Hold the group as a whole accountable.** Running a business is a dance, so you need to make sure that the movement is smooth! Everyone should be working toward the same goal, whatever that goal may be. There is a saying that you are only as strong as your weakest link. Yes, a weak link is a problem, but ask yourself why there is a weak link in the first place. The weak link might not be at fault on his own, but rather might be failing because there is a hidden weakness somewhere else in the chain that is affecting him.

**The shopkeeper should practice what he or she preaches.** The shopkeeper needs to be on the floor taking orders, talking to customers, cooking, selling, designing, grooming dogs...and generally being a part of the team. He or she needs to be constantly demonstrative to the staff regarding how things should be done. If you want things done right, then you better be damn willing to do them right yourself.

**Be sure to chart objectives and review them on a timely basis.** Name them, categorize them, colour code them, and plot them. Clearly define what it is that you expect from your customer service people. You must make sure to lay out the expectations clearly and allow your staff to have access to the list on a regular basis. Having this information allows them to monitor and gauge whether they have made good on the promise to the customer. The promise, the goal, the vision, often gets lost in the chaos of day-to-day operations. It is important to pause the dance once in a while to re-establish the ultimate promise by referring to the list.

**Lastly, be ready for eventualities as much as possible.** Or at least be willing to address them. We opened our café on a Thursday thinking that we were ready and that we had everything in place. Funny enough, despite the planning, the lists, the calculations, and our strategy, we simply weren't prepared for everything that happened. Our well-thought-out plans backfired on us a little bit. It was a humbling and extremely exciting experience all at the same time. It took being open and running for a while before we finally got the formula down. We learned a lot, and there was a lot of trial and error along the way.

I have found that this rings true across all types of businesses and across all types of industries; things will go wrong. Big things will go wrong and little things will go wrong. But as long as you are willing to react to them, work through them, and handle them, things can be turned around. Some in the dance will dive in with extra support; others will need to take your hand, but together you will be strong. You will find your rhythm, and you will keep dancing.

# CHAPTER
# TWO

. . . . . . . . . . . . . . . . . . . . . . . . . . . . .

# DANCE LESSONS

. . . . . . . . . . . . . . . . . . . . . . . . . . . . .

## PROVIDING CUSTOMER SERVICE TRAINING

**T**raining is the foundation of good customer service. *Period*. Let's delve further into this topic because proper training is the key to great customer service, which is, in turn, the key to success.

Recently, I've been spending a considerable amount of time in Austin, Texas. There, I've had one of the most delightful customer service experiences—and I've travelled a lot! Let me show you what I mean by not needing to be one of the giants to practice the fundamentals and succeed like they do. There is an eatery called Torchy's Tacos that is a staple in Austin. There are many locations, and I noticed that a new location was going up near where I was staying. I paid close attention to the construction of the new location. It was fun to watch because each of Torchy's buildings has a unique '50s retro style architecture. Once it opened, large lines could be seen out front at almost all times of the day. Customers apparently didn't mind the line because they said that the place inside was spacious, the food was great, and there were plenty of tables. For that reason, I decided to try it out. That and the fact that I love tacos. Who doesn't? So this was going to be a serious checking out.

I visited Torchy's newest location, and immediately I knew what all the hype was about. I got to the front of the line at the counter and was greeted by a lovely gentleman. Instantly, I forgot about my wait to get there; he made me feel important because he was completely focused on me. Even his body language told me that I was the center of that moment, as he was leaning into me, making eye contact, and smiling. Most importantly, he shut up and listened. I asked him to help me with the menu as I warned him that I despise mayo and it must not be in my food. He laughed as I told him that it seemed to be an American staple, especially in the South!

The man at the counter recommended two choices and kindly assured me that there would be no mayo (unlike the reaction I usually get from my kids over this issue) and also explained that they were indeed great choices (unlike options I am usually left with). I explained I hadn't been there before. He smiled and told me to take a numbered flag and sit wherever I like. I proceeded to the bar with my laptop to write and felt pleasantly happy. I was happy because that man knew his job and his product and cared. I encounter employees all of the time who are not familiar with their products (why don't they know?!), and it's such a *basic* integral part of great service.

As I started writing on my laptop, a lovely girl behind the bar came to me and asked how I was. She clearly saw what I was doing, and she went out of her way to point out an outlet near me so that if I needed to charge the laptop, she would plug it in for me. I was kind of shocked. I looked at her and asked if she liked cold weather, because we needed more people like her back in Canada.

When my food arrived, it looked exactly like it did in the pictures. The man delivering my food set it down, waited for the "thumbs-up" and left. He didn't interrupt my meal or try to take away my plate before I was finished. This is crucial to me—a pet peeve really. I don't like it when servers come by to clear before I am finished, or when they move as if they are trying to get me out faster.

On a side note, this is a subject that we train extensively on at the café; one example is to always wait to clear any plates until *all* diners are clearly finished. And if you are not sure, ask before you grab. Go to the best restaurants and observe. Dishes are never removed while someone is still eating, which is incredibly rude. "Reaching and clearing" while anyone is still enjoying their experience is a professional no-no unless you are asked to. It's putting common practices like this in place, and adhering to them, that separates you from your competition in the "right" way. If you want to be like the big people, then behave as if you are. Having a professional attitude does not cost extra. But I digress...

I was inspired, at that point, to write up an observation of Torchy's Tacos as I took the time to make some observations. I wrote a short page on what was working and why. Here is what I saw, here is the dance that was working: There were plenty of staff, but they weren't running into each other or the customers. Each staff member had a distinct, separate function, and each one knew exactly what it was. Servers never really had to leave their stations, and they were able to move customers easily. There were specific people there to move the food, and they never touched money or anything else that is questionably clean. My tacos, with no mayo, arrived fresh and hot and not altogether untimely—well worth the wait. As a whole, it was a grade A experience. Most importantly, all their customers were relaxed and smiling.

I could tell that, despite not being open for very long, the staff had all received extensive, appropriate, and intensive training. No one operated on autopilot. They smiled graciously, were humble, and attentive. There was nothing by rote. They addressed me with the appropriate title (ma'am and Ms.). I asked random questions of more than one staff member, and they all answered and acted as a team; they moved at the same tune, all in step with each other.

As I left Torchy's, I passed the gentleman from the counter outside by the parking lot. He stopped me and asked me if I enjoyed my tacos, and with a nice smile asked if there was any mayo on them. I laughed because I was happy he'd remembered! I relayed that I critique customer service, and I showed him what I wrote up about them. I felt his pride. It was important to let him know because they had taken very good care of me, and I wanted to be a great customer in return. When it goes well, your customers will respond accordingly.

The aforementioned anecdote speaks to the crucial importance of proper training! I can't hammer this home enough: *training is the key to a quality customer experience.* I can tell when employees have been trained well because every employee treats every customer the same and can answer all of their questions in a satisfactory way. Remember, customers are always talking bad about businesses that have provided them with a similarly terrible experience. You can prevent this from happening to your business by providing training!

### THIS BEGS THE QUESTION...WHAT IS THE KEY TO PROPER TRAINING?

First, it is important to lead by example. The person who first taught me to become the best employee I could ever be was the sales manager in my entry job into customer service. He led by example. He taught me, listened to me, and helped me when I needed it, but most importantly, he was his own best employee. This same person would later become my business partner.

Second, share knowledge, experience, and desire with your employees. Hopefully, some of that drive will rub off on them, and they will want to learn as much as they can from you. Fair warning, treat them well; you don't want to train your competition's future employees.

Third, communication is key. Never, ever talk down to your staff during training or any time "on the floor," It is easy to get frustrated, but remember, you didn't know something before you learned it for the first time...nobody did. Listen, listen, listen to your staff. They have a question? Answer it. They have subsequent questions? Answer them too! Set aside specific times throughout the day (or week, or month, etc.) to talk: morning, noon, or at close of business. Of course, make sure that they know that although you are available, there are such things as inappropriate times to talk. Unless it's an emergency, don't stop the dance midway through to talk about something that can wait. You all will learn together what works over time.

When communicating, ask your employees what you could do better or what they feel like they are lacking in order to do their jobs. I always made sure that I did this in all of my businesses, and it created trusting and open relationships. It does not mean you will necessarily make changes or adaptations, but you are open to considering it.

In that vein, ask your employees straight out what they think about the operation and how things are handled. You may not choose to take their advice, but simply asking makes them feel important and gives them value. I ask my employees for thoughts, ideas, opinions, and then I just let them talk. It's amazing what comes out of them. And they would know; they have to handle our most important asset: our customers.

Next, follow-up. Buy yourself and all staff notebooks. Make notes, log times, and jot down dates, and be creative with it. It is very important to catalogue everything. Have your staff write down things that they want to discuss with you. Also, have them write down issues with customers. Make sure that they include the names of customers. You should also use this logbook to index repeated wrongdoings of staff. If you need to let someone go because the employee has refused to change his or her behaviour, then you will have a written record of that person's mistakes. We had a girl working at the café who refused to follow the rules of the establishment. I talked to her many times, but she refused to change. Thankfully, I wrote all of her missteps down and so had a thorough list that I could refer to. I was able to show her each questionable instance, and it gave me credibility. That logbook should be on your person, or easily available at all times. Write things down, and when you sit down to talk at the end of the day, you can reference the information.

This process of sitting down and revisiting events your service staff has logged is important because it shows that you care. By doing this, you are accomplishing three things. First, you are telling your employees that you care about what they have to say. This empowers them. It also transfers the right to care; it makes them feel like they should also concern themselves with customers' feelings. This is an important thing because they, of course, have the most contact with customers. This speaks to the situation I encountered at Torchy's. That employee cared enough to go out of his way to ask me how everything went for me. I have no doubt that that man sat down with his manager later that day and told him about his interaction with me.

Second, this engenders a relationship between shopkeeper and employee that is a succinct one. If your employee feels that you care for him, then he might feel as though he should care for you. It is good for your employees to feel camaraderie, which confirms that you are both in it together.

Lastly, it allows the employee an opportunity to enter the world of his or her shopkeeper. Daily conversations with your staff will allow them to get a glimpse into that world. This is a good way for you, as a shopkeeper, to scout for the talent amongst your staff. You can really see who wants to be a part of the upper management, and when promotions or spots open up, it will help you have a better idea of who can fill those positions.

Give your staff the time they need in training. We can change the tempo of the dance. We can speed it up, change the rhythm, or slow it down, but we cannot pause the song. So, when you are training, slow the tempo to allow your staff to get the moves down. Therefore, you won't have to stop the music later on when the tempo increases and the lights go up.

### RESOURCES TO USE FOR TRAINING

There are many resources that you should utilize in order to enhance your training process. First and foremost, you should gift your staff this book. Use this book as a tool to empower your employees. Have them read it and fill it out and then have a conversation about it.

Apply situations that they have experienced at your business to ones that are discussed here. By talking about specific situations, real or made up, in your experience, or in theirs, you can discuss the appropriate way to handle things so that when situations arise again, that employee won't necessarily have to refer back to you. He or she may, hopefully, deal with the situation all on his or her own. Start small. Give them common situations. You should know what a common situation is in your business. Especially since now everyone has a logbook.

I highly recommend this book as one of your primary training tools, but you should also supplement it with workshops and videos. I am and have always been a huge fan of workshops. Back in the day, before the Internet, or the widespread use of videos, we held seminars. For all you Millennials, seminars are workshops that usually last a day or two. They were informational, dedicated to a particular order of business, and designed for maximum learning impact. The trend, of course, has transformed into more of a Big Name, "rah-rah," pump-up type of atmosphere. They certainly have their benefits, and they focus a lot on spirit. I personally feel as though these big densely packed seminars with celebrity speakers tend to be more general and may not necessarily speak to you or your company. Rather, any given speaker just extolls his or her own virtues and methods, and look, don't you just wanna be them! But what happens when you get home and the giant speakers aren't there to pound the blood in your ears and neither are the multitudes standing around you?

Are they creating a positive, innovative, educational, and creative atmosphere where personal moments of clarity are possible? That's for you to decide. Of course, there are exceptions, as with anything. Speaking of moments of clarity, I do love the more humble motivators who care more about you finding the strength to be fearless and to keep trying and to become leaders in your own right and in your passions. And today, of course, you don't necessarily need to travel to access them, although that is a good idea if you can, at least once. What people do need to seek out are smaller, more intimate workshops that are specific to their business, but also to their philosophy and energy and their own prescription for success. Think TED Talks. By the way, if you haven't seen them, get into them.

Available to us are a plethora of speakers who all claim that they can "enlighten," "enhance," "train," and "motivate" us. These types are all *New York Times* best sellers with glossy book covers, incredibly flashy websites, and personas to match. They all call themselves the "leader" and certainly, it seems, that they have the necessary credentials. To me, they all look the same.

I don't think all of the principles touted by these old-school thinkers should apply to the Millennial generation. The last thing that these excessively creative and forward thinking Millennials want to do is regress to utilizing old methods.

For that reason, I say that each shopkeeper should assess his own needs and do his homework online to investigate more unique and pointed avenues of learning.

My personal style is more grassroots. I like to attend classy, simpler conferences and workshops where I come away with tools and respect for others who understand challenges as I do, or provide powerful messages in a quiet, simplistic way in order to focus on the speaker or material.

There are great Canadian resources online such as the Canadian Association of Professional Speakers, Keynote Speakers of Canada, and ProSpeakers: Canada's Professional Keynote and Conference Speakers. A wealth of information can be gathered from these forums in areas such as time management, customer service, sales, and team/business development.

In the very early days of my career, I went to a workshop on customer service that remains with me today. All of us attendees were sitting in a conference room with about fifty chairs. The leader of the seminar opened with a story of an interaction he had had just moments before with the organizer from the hotel. While setting up, he had asked her if there was a phone in the conference room. He was referring to those big clunky ugly beige contraptions you may have seen before that plug into a landline in the wall—this *was* the '80s. She responded by saying to him "Oh yes, yes, of course, I'll go get one," and then ran out of the door. He paused the story, looked out into the crowd, and asked us what her answer should have been. Looking around it was clear to me that nobody knew the answer. Well, I knew what had gone wrong and so I answered. The woman had simply assumed that he was asking her for a phone instead of asking him what he needed. Her only answer should have been, "That depends on whether you would like one in here or not." Then she should have proceeded to make arrangements either way. He smiled and nodded his head. It turned out that he was asking her because he didn't want a phone in the conference room. He said that the last thing that he needed was a phone ringing and interrupting him in the middle of his seminar. She had failed to determine what the customer wanted and had assumed incorrectly.

That was the point that I knew that I was in the right business.

I realized during that seminar, after looking around at all of the people who hadn't raised their hand, just how much there is to understand about customer service. And it takes a specific kind of thought process to be good at it. This is why attending workshops is so important. You need to be around skilled people so that you can continually learn in order to keep yourself fresh and dynamic. I suggest offering to pay for your staff to attend workshops at least once a year. It allows them the ability to stay apace with trends and even look toward the future. Investing in your employees is an important function of any good boss.

Take this in: A man watches another man set up a little shop to sell homemade candles. He does very well based on the volume attending his business. So the first man says to himself, "Hey, I can do that; that's so simple. I can make candles." So he too opens a little shop and within three months he is closed. Why? Because there is a big difference between knowing how to make candles and knowing how to sell candles.

Utilize the Internet as well. Limitless resources for training, learning, and networking are readily available to anyone at any time by just connecting to Wi-Fi. By taking advantage of online resources, you will also be able to keep up with the rapidly transforming landscape of the twenty-first century.

One of my favourite online resources is videos of talks (I love that they are no longer referred to as speeches) by Dr. Brené Brown, PhD. Dr. Brown defines herself as a researcher and storyteller. She has two very popular, very powerful, TED Talks called "The Power of Vulnerability" and "Listening to Shame." The former is the fourth most viewed Ted Talk across all categories. I recommend both of these videos to my readers and to all of my friends and employees. Her message is a universal one; it addresses the propensity of humans to constantly feel as though we are failing. Dr. Brown states that vulnerability is the birthplace of creativity and innovation.

I received a call one day from a friend who was in tears because she had only been at work, her own private business, for two hours, yet three huge problems, her mistakes, had already come up. I worked it out with her, gave her words of encouragement, but also discussed action if she determined she had to close for the day. She went on and worked through the problems and ended up having a record-breaking day. From this, I feel that while we are striving for excellence in what we do, mistakes can seem like failures. There is a world of difference between setting your personal bar at 100 percent and achieving 90 percent, and setting it at 80 percent and achieving 90. Vulnerability is an essential part of being successful; getting it right the first time is not. Allow yourself room to deal with problems that will inevitably happen.

There are also a variety of online courses that you can take during your extra time and at your own pace to complement what you learn in the workplace. They can be especially helpful for those of us who haven't had the opportunity to complete secondary education. Local colleges often have distance learning programs that offer correspondence or print-based courses. You may want to consider a marketing course or even one in creative writing. Public speaking or negotiation classes are also great tools to have in your back pocket.

There is another great resource that so many people overlook: the library! Yes, that old bastion of society that unfortunately remains a symbol of yesteryear. There you can find many helpful materials including in-depth books on a variety of business and self-help topics. A particular book that I recommend is called *The Rules of Work* by Richard Templar. It has been in publication for ten years or so but remains a concise and helpful resource for shopkeepers and employees alike.

I was inspired to create my own workplace mottos that can be frequently heard around my house and in my businesses. They are "Double C" and "Double D," "Double C" stands for Clear and Concise. Clear and concise are the ways in which your employees should speak to your customers. "Double D" stands for Dignity and Decorum. These are the ways in which I expect my staff to behave.

Use your competition as another resource for training

exercises. I took the café employees to a fine dining experience where we talked about what was going well and what wasn't. An experience like that is just as informational as a workshop, but it allowed my employees to apply their skills to the real world. I had them critique the service, and then we applied it to their own work. Although the level of service was much higher than we require from the employees at the café (given the fact that it was a fine dining restaurant), I wanted to show them that there was meaning and importance at every level.

Look to other companies that you admire or that are successful as case studies. Learn about their history, their journey, and where they are now.

Mine your network. People in your industry are experienced and well versed, so utilize their knowledge. You should also look to your boss, as he or she is a primary member of your network. Make sure to approach him or her at an appropriate time with a good question, and most times, they will be happy to answer. This is the human connection that cannot be replicated by any other resource. This is especially important for the Millennial generation to understand; although you have countless tools, the best source of information is the people around you. Don't forget the human touch.

A logbook is another crucial tool to use for training purposes. Your logbook is your heartbeat. It will allow you to refer back to crucial moments in your training. Keeping a thorough record is necessary in order to continue to learn about how to perfect your process. Keep your logbook at hand at all times. Buy your staff logbooks as well.

Utilizing as many resources as you can is important, but make sure that you set high standards for the information that you take away.

. . .

Let's use one real-life example to discuss what went wrong and what went right in the training process.

The banking industry has always had a formal, institutional air about it. It is important that banks have this type of reputation because they are relied upon to handle money. Money dictates our present and the trajectory of our future, so it is exceedingly important for customers to feel safe with their banking institutions. Banking employees need to act according to this reputation and thus must consistently offer professional customer service.

My current banking institution has proven its reliable reputation by treating me in an exceptionally professional manner. The bank is clear, truthful, and helpful to me.

Even the title that it gives its customer service representatives speaks to this. The bank refers to them as client associates. In my mind, my "client associate" is there for me; it's a personal feeling, as compared to a "customer service representative" who is there for me and thousands of other people. All customers, especially in banking, are unique and have different requirements, needs, dreams, hopes, desires, and financial standings. Times have necessitated personal attention and putting the customer at the centre. It has become corporate culture. Decades ago it was less competitive and more "one size fits all." But competition has changed this, and suitably for the better. My client associate goes above and beyond in a way that I am assured that I am understood. The woman who handles my finances calls me regularly, especially if she doesn't hear from me in a while; she is very responsive, follows up with me, never hides anything, and treats me like an individual...because I am.

I knew someone who was a financial advisor in the '90s. He ended up skipping town when things started to go south in the market. Before he did, however, I remember him complaining to me that his phone wouldn't stop ringing. He was so frustrated with it and that was his reason for leaving. Well, of course your phone won't stop ringing! I wanted to shout that it was reasonable for people to be calling him because they trusted him, and had lost their savings, their children's college funds, and their retirement accounts! He should have known that because of the service that he was in, he had to be able to take the good calls and the bad calls.

I love Kelly, the woman who handles a very important financial aspect of my life, for that reason. She even goes beyond because she never fails to have a plan for me *before* we speak. That indicates that she sits down, thinks everything through, and writes it all out. What does she have? A plan! With good news, she has a plan. With bad news, she has a plan. It makes me feel calm, and I harbour a feeling that I'm taken care of. But not everyone is a Kelly. I would be satisfied with someone who called to tell me that they would think more about it, gather information, and schedule a follow-up call.

To me, this type of service is fantastic, but there was a time I never knew it existed. Back in 1984, I was using one bank and my fiancé at the time was using another. I noticed how differently his bank treated him compared to mine. He could walk into the bank, and everyone would know his name. People asked how he was doing, what he needed, and what they could do for him. I was shocked!

I had been going to my small community bank for several years. I had even paid off a student loan through them. I had put all of my money in their hands, but when I walked in, they didn't even know who I was. I was never greeted, and I never received the level of care that I saw his bank giving him. So at that time before there were emails, I wrote a handwritten letter chronicling my concerns and handed it in to my institution. Shortly thereafter, I walked into my bank, and it was a whole different atmosphere. The tellers were actually smiling and calling people by name and taking their time to make sure each customer was properly serviced. I can't ever know for sure, but I believe that it was my letter that changed the face of that particular branch!

This story occurred at the cusp of a new era in customer service. Before the cusp, we were still muddling in the grey area of customer service that had replaced the homey feel consistent with the earlier era. The other side of the cusp—post '90s—was a time of stepping up in order to offer the best customer service that we could. To me, the defining characteristic of this movement is embodied in a phrase that all customer service people are trained to utter at the end of each interaction: "Did you find everything you were looking for?" When this practice first began, I thought it was lovely. I felt that whenever I was asked this question, I was being looked after and certainly someone cared. Unfortunately, this practice has turned sour. It feels as though it is now uttered simply as a formality.

Over and over, I hear this question asked in a rote, passive manner. I know that most customers always respond in the affirmative ("Yes I did, thanks."), but I wonder what would happen if a customer answered, "No, I did not." I wonder if the employee would even know how to help the customer, or to direct him or her appropriately to someone who may be able to, or to handle the lineup of other customers not wanting to now be held up further.

Sometimes, I purposely answer in the negative just to find out what will happen, mostly at the larger establishments with a dozen or so checkouts as the smaller ones are usually very helpful. When asked, I reply that I didn't find everything I needed. Most of the time, the employee just stands there and stares, as if they don't know what my statement is regarding, and wait for *me* to elaborate. This is what I mean by rote; they are speaking their dialogue as part of a practice or out of habit, not a concern. Sometimes I answer "no" in the same tone as theirs, with a smile, and the response, if I get one, is usually "OK great."

My kids roll their eyes at me when I do this, but I sincerely think it is an important practice. Customer service representatives need to be challenged to stay alert and to stay refreshed. Recently, at a small airport, I had decided to hunt down a local t-shirt and went into a one-manned boutique. I did approach the young woman first and ask if she had any, and she informed me they did not. Not five minutes later I brought to the checkout the one I decided to settle for instead. As she rings up the purchase doesn't she ask if I found everything I was looking for. I simply looked at her, opened my mouth to speak but nothing came out, and soon we were both laughing. She even admitted to me that she does that simply out of habit and without paying attention.

. . .

We've discussed the importance of proper training in customer service and talked about an example of an industry that is built upon these good practices. Now I want to examine five tips for when you want to practice correct customer service training in real-life scenarios.

**1. PRACTICE, PRACTICE, AND PRACTICE SOME MORE.** Keep doing it! Practice even after you have opened. Practice when you are open and operating. New things will come up, so make sure you are prepared and have covered everything you can. Be sure to practice dry runs as well! The art of the dry run is beautiful and never goes out of style!

**2. BE MINDFUL OF WHAT OTHER RESOURCES YOUR EMPLOYEES USE FOR TRAINING.** Make sure that you have given out your recommended training tools. Provide your employees with a seminar of your choosing. Gift them a book that you like. Suggest specific videos on YouTube that you personally refer to. Lastly, check in with them to make sure that they understand the material.

**3. BE AN EXAMPLE.** Be there. Be there. Be there. Let them watch you in action. Get on the floor with them. There's nothing better or more satisfying for the shopkeeper than to feel that he or she is a part of that action. Again, do not assume that your employees can work like you do. So show them how it's done! They need to see the dance the way you want it done!

**4. GIVE PRAISE.** Do it in front of the customer. Employees love getting praise that way; it is the ultimate gift for them. I will sometimes even address the customer and point to my staff and say, "Isn't so-and-so awesome? He is doing such a great job today. Thank goodness we have him during the lunch rush!" Give your employee a high five without stopping the dance. Send an email, or send a text; give them a gold star. Even the very little things matter.

I also like to give praise at times where my staff has clearly gone out of their way to be helpful. If someone has the guts to come up to me and say, "You know what I was thinking? We should change A and B and then the issue with C might be better," I have to give them praise. Even if it isn't a great idea, I am always impressed with that initiative.

On this note, I don't recommend using the employee of the month system. I believe that it is an old-fashioned, outdated system that engenders inherent tension within the team. I believe that businesses had good intentions when putting it into place. They probably believed that it would inspire people to want to excel. I believe, however, that it simply inspires animosity between co-workers. I can speak from experience that it certainly created a different dynamic that had a negative effect when I was part of a sales team. My staff is a team, and that particular way of awarding is for the individual. As with anything, there are exceptions; it is up to you to find and use discretion. There is a fine line between encouraging teamwork (we really are in this together for the success of the business) and encouraging jealousy (I'm not even going to bother. Why should I?).

**5. REWARD THE TEAM.** If I want to give a material reward, I will buy them lunch. I have found that it goes far. Lunch, to me, represents a casual time when I can really bond with my employees and offer them a relaxed and casual experience to just sit and chat. It lasts just long enough, and it makes them feel important in a simple way. And, of course, there are times when dinner is more appropriate, as with managers or team leaders.

Quite a few years back, when I was a part of a sales team

newly put together—seven in total, six men and myself—each week we would measure the top salesperson by keeping tally on a big board on our sales floor. Sometimes on a Friday, we would add up the numbers and reward the highest in gross sales. You can imagine the big push from everyone that day. Being the brash young salesperson that I was, I usually kicked butt. The prize was a hundred dollars. I inevitably used the money to treat my co-workers and myself to lunch with it. Hey, a hundred bucks went quite a long way then. We celebrated an awesome week collectively. I succeeded but I didn't need to walk above them.

There was much spirit, drive, and camaraderie amongst us. On that note, don't allow one person to hog the dance floor, encourage everyone to dance. You want to make heroes out of your entire staff. Some will outshine over time, it's natural, but they all need your support. It will come back to you tenfold.

It is important to incentivize employees to practice great customer service. You can do this by making sure that they are aware that they can advance their careers by doing so. Use the following list to clearly outline how your employees can advance their careers, or in general their success, through solid customer service.

**1. BE A CONSISTENT WORKER!** Do the best job you can 100 percent of the time. Notice that I didn't say that you need to be perfect all of the time. Rather, *do your best* all of the time. There is a huge difference.

It always shows when you are doing the best you can. Everyone has to deal with circumstances in their lives, but even when there are personal setbacks, try your best! It shows when you try. When your shopkeeper sees that, he or she will be more forgiving if you are a little tired or have made mistakes that are unlike you.

Make sure that you never sacrifice your own integrity for the sake of someone else. Don't cover for anyone in a dishonest way. Don't lie.

**2. TAKE CHARGE**, take ownership, and show interest in the success of the company. Show that you actually care about it, and your work will reflect that.

**3. YOUR NUMBER-ONE DUTY**, of course, is always to focus on the customers' needs within the boundaries of what you're allowed to do.

**4. SMILE.** No fake smiles, no frowns, no huffing, no eye rolls, no sighing. There is nothing wrong with injecting pleasure into the work environment. You can laugh and have fun and be funny! For the love of God, put some music on once in a while. Sing.

**5. DO MORE THAN JUST TAKE THE ORDER.** You've got to follow through. You must be sure that your product or service actually gets to the customer and that it gets to him in an appropriate time and the manner in which he has been promised.

**6. LEARN AS MUCH AS YOU CAN ABOUT THE COMPANY.** Everybody should start in the mailroom. By that, I don't always mean the actual mailroom. It's an expression from the old days when corporations stood twenty stories high and the mailroom was located in the basement. Starting your learning within the basic framework of the company gives you knowledge from the ground up. Climb the floors by showing your interest in learning about the way things work. It will also help you gain valuable insight into the company's philosophies, principles, and strategies. Talk to people, ask them questions, and pay attention.

**7. OBSERVE WHAT IS WORKING** within your own job and then assess what improvements can be made. You're the person who is there working every day. You're the one who is interacting with the customer. What have you found that works? Did you get a lot of complaints today? Were all of the complaints about the same thing? Where can improvements be made? If you want to advance your career, think about these things. Don't be shy about talking with your superiors about any worries you may have. Flat out tell them. I have a great story a family friend shared with me that speaks to this concept.

When he cooks hams for the holidays, he always cuts the end off of it before he bakes it. One day, his daughter came to him and asked why he did that. She was told that's how his mom did it. So the daughter then asked her grandmother why she cut the end of her hams off. She was then told that she did it because *her* mother did. So his daughter went to her great-grandmother and asked her why she cut the ends off of her hams.

Her great-grandmother told her that she did it because, "It was the only way to fit it in the only pan that I had!" For decades, we were all wasting a perfectly good piece of ham and weren't even sure why!

Sometimes, the ingenious one is the one who asks the obvious questions.

**8. DON'T JUST DO WHAT'S EXPECTED OF YOU.** Don't just take into consideration the task at hand. Think about the bigger picture: What can you do now while you are just standing around? What needs to be done in the long run?

**9. THINK ABOUT HOW TO INCREASE BUSINESS.** Use creativity to both solve development problems and find new customers. Consider the current circumstances and think outside the box in order to find solutions. Use outside talents in order to help inside the business. If you are a really talented digital artist, and your company is rebranding and looking for a new logo, submit your work! Whether you are in sales, or HR, if you have a talent, don't be afraid to use it!

**10. TALK ABOUT WHAT ELSE THE COMPANY HAS TO OFFER.** As managers and owners, we love it when someone asks what the requirements are for moving up into a specific position. If Amanda in sales is going on maternity leave and you want to know what it would take to fill her slot, ask! Just asking and showing curiosity means that you're halfway there.

**11. NEVER BE LAZY.** Don't assume your job ends because your role has specific outlines. "That's not my job" doesn't exist if you want to offer great customer service. If you find yourself thinking, "I did my job, and so now I'm just going to sit here and watch my two slow co-workers finish their tasks," then you need to check yourself. Don't sit there with your arms crossed staring at them. Walk over to the two and offer, "Okay, what are we doing here guys? Let's get this done."

In more than one business, I have defined the need for and instituted a "floater." The floater's job is to simply go from place to place wherever he or she is needed to help out. The job, really, is to make sure that the dance can keep on, can flow, and everyone is aware of the role. The relief is palpable at times and, when visible to the customer, the extra layer of care doesn't get past them. If you are an employee who is always looking to help out, you will be spotted a mile away. To add to this, be on time or early.

**12. DON'T WATCH THE CLOCK.** We all do sometimes, but please don't make it obvious. If you have a specific reason, like you need to pick up kids from preschool, it's okay to be wary of the time. Otherwise, please refrain from this practice. As we all know, it only makes time go slower! Instead, show you are focused on the importance of the job.

**13. EXPRESS THE TEAMWORK ETHIC.** I love when someone steps up and takes the initiative to drive teamwork and communication.

**14. LASTLY, LISTEN WHEN SOMEONE HIGHER UP SPEAKS.** Pay attention when in an informal setting; they are handing out free advice. Don't glaze over, or start looking at your phone when in a formal environment. Staying focused on them is professional, always. We see you. If you are in the middle of an important work task and can't give them your eyes, there is no harm in writing them a note later to tell them that you were indeed listening.

In the end, providing good customer service benefits not only the shopkeeper and the customer, but the employee as well.

# CHAPTER
# THREE

. . . . . . . . . . . . . . . . . . . . . . . . . . . . . .

# MAY I HAVE
# THIS DANCE?

. . . . . . . . . . . . . . . . . . . . . . . . . . . . . .

## CUSTOMER SERVICE
## RULES AND ETIQUETTE

**B**efore I get any further into this chapter, I want to share with you a little nursery rhyme that I've adopted and modernized. It goes like this:

*Whether a lawyer, a baker, a candlestick maker, whether you're on the street, in a shop, over the phone or online, your formula should always align.*

I hope I've caught your attention, dear reader, because I engineered that silly rhyme to make a salient point; regardless of what you do, or who you are, everyone must follow a formula for success. The customer service principles outlined next are applicable and compulsory across all industries.

This chapter outlines key rules and etiquette in customer service that apply across industries. I want to specifically speak to how these rules should be communicated to your employees.

Regardless of if you are selling to a customer in person or over the phone, proper hygiene is exceedingly important. First impressions are everything. This is simply how the mind works; we see and we think we know. We trust what our eyes are telling us. Thus the customer assesses what he sees before anything else. This is why companies spend massive amounts on visual advertising and marketing. This is why we house our businesses in lovely buildings to create inviting atmospheres. This is why we spend money on pleasant-looking uniforms and require dress codes. Their first visual impression is the most important. Why is it so important? Because the customer will translate his first impression of your customer service representative onto your company. If your employee is unhygienic, this does not relay a very pretty picture of your product or service.

By "good hygiene" I mean good personal hygiene *and* good business hygiene. Personal hygiene includes requiring employees to regularly wash their hands. Make sure that there is a sink and soap close by and, if possible, have your employees wash their hands in front of the customer. This adds that extra level of accountability that does not exist behind closed doors. Of course, these rules apply mostly to the hospitality industries, but should be practiced across all industries, because we should all be mindful of each other as well.

If you are handling money or food, specifically, you should take even further precaution by wearing gloves. In addition, I want to speak to the issue of staff having their personal phones on their person. There is no need for touching their phones at any point when they are on duty. The bacteria! I swear that the Millennial generation will be the healthiest generation and the most immune to monumental disease because of their attachment to their phones! The advancement of humanity is a beautiful thing, but *please* don't keep those phones anywhere near your hands or face when you are working.

Keep yourself tidy. You hair should be pulled back if the job necessitates. You must also be consistent with your uniform; wear it properly every day. I have a huge problem with employees who cheat with their apparel concerning what is appropriate according to the job requirements. And please don't run around in clothing that clearly hasn't been washed since the Clinton administration!

Lastly, being well groomed is an essential part of personal hygiene. Wash your hair, brush your teeth, wash your face; stay fresh. Truly, it's not much to ask. We are all adults here. Unfortunately, many people still can't be bothered to cover the basics.

Good hygiene is also important behind the scenes. If

you are dealing with customers online or over the phone, hygiene is still crucial because customers can sense it, believe it or not. It is also just common courtesy for the benefit of your fellow employees, bosses, or anyone else that you are around!

Proper hygiene for your business is important as well. By this I am referring to the sanitation and health of the workplace that you have provided for your staff. Are the public areas in your brick-and-mortar clean and tidy? Have you provided a clean and comfortable place to work? Are there bathrooms that are readily available to your staff and, if required, your customers? Is there somewhere that is obviously identifiable as a place for your employees to wash up? You, as a shopkeeper, must make sure that the tools are there for your staff to make your environment a hygienic one. By giving them these tools, you are allowing your staff the ability to keep things visibly functional, clean, and organized. Layout procedures that your staff can follow to make sure that the place is always set up and organized. When something is amiss, work through it with a smile.

### BODY LANGUAGE AND EYE CONTACT

Speaking of working through it with a smile, it is important to be cognizant of your body language. Proper eye contact is a crucial aspect and an essential part of any interaction with a customer. Making eye contact with your customer upon his entering your business tells him that you acknowledge him. It shows your customers that yes, indeed, they will be looked after. I don't care how busy you are, you must pause and take a moment to give the customer your attention. Open your face up to welcome this person with a smile. It is far more relaxing for the customer knowing that he's been spotted in the event that you are very busy with other tasks at hand.

The principle of "eye contact" should also be considered when speaking on the phone with the customer. I think of it more as the "lean in," I can actually hear it when the person on the other line is sitting up and leaning into our conversation. If you try speaking while slouched and then try speaking while sitting up straight, you will see how differently you project your voice. Try it now! By leaning in, the customer service rep is removing all other distractions from his perimeter. It is amazing how voice and attitude changes when you are leaning in versus laying on your back or putting your feet up. When speaking over the phone, this allows you to direct the conversation. It is the correlating component to eye contact, which allows you to initiate and drive conversations. And let's not forget the most important thing: it allows you to "listen."

## NO DISTRACTIONS

No distractions. Stay focused. This means no personal phone or anything else near you or on your desk that might distract you! Do not let your mind wander. Stay at the task at hand. Remember that no job is greater than answering to the needs of the customer. If your fellow employees are constantly off task, or are always wanting to chat, be mindful and tell them that you will be happy to do these things or listen to them after your shift. If you've ever had to suffer through the grocery checkout as an extra pair of hands shows up to help and she is, without looking down, grabbing and throwing your precious goods into the bag like she is the starting warm-up because the real reason she came is to parlay to your cashier all about the latest issue from last night, then you know what I mean.

Make sure that you have the proper tools to stay focused. If you have blood sugar problems, let a snack tag along to get you through. There is nothing wrong with that. Keep a bottle of water around to stay hydrated. If you need to get up every hour or so and walk around for a couple of minutes, then by all means, take that time to refocus. You must identify ahead of time what you require to keep focused.

## BE CONSISTENT

Be consistent. This word has come up over and over again for a reason. As a shopkeeper, you must make sure that your service people are consistent. Make sure that they are always dancing. Make sure that everyone is moving toward the same objective by using similar patterns and behaviours. This doesn't mean that everyone has to be the exact same; we encourage varied personalities. Consistency across the board means being consistent in your work progress, attitude, and ideals. Consistency applies day-to-day and minute-to-minute. Sometimes consistency cannot be achieved. At those times, give your employee a pep talk, or a soda. As for the latter, well, it's amazing what offering or handing them one can do to bring it all home again.

### FOLLOW-UP

Your job isn't done when the customer walks away with the product or service. Businesses rely on keeping customers, not just getting them. Therefore, keeping service at the highest level even after the sale is good practice. By follow-up, I don't mean asking the customer if they found everything they needed. That can become nothing more than a rote, meaningless statement, as I mentioned earlier. Besides, you want to define and design your own signature. Go beyond it. For instance, if something went amiss, follow-up to apologize. Don't be afraid to humble yourself. Many people are afraid to admit mistakes. Their reaction is to push the customer away as fast as possible. Never hide, never dodge fault. Don't look away from the mistakes, because they may just get worse. There is some-thing inherently charming about telling a customer, "Wow, I'm so sorry. I can't believe I just did this. But, I caught it!" Ask the customer how you can make it up to him. Playing the blame game is even worse. Never blame your co-workers (i.e., pass the buck) or the customer herself. In these cases, all you have to do is say, "I'm so sorry, I must have misunderstood what you wanted. You're right, I didn't hear you say that."

I have a particular story that speaks to the importance of the follow-up. There is a small, family-run community market near my house. This is a place where everyone knows each other's name, and most, if not all, of the cus-tomers are recurring. They have my ideal products at this market: juicy peaches and fresh eggs and beautiful local vegetables. I really love it because they are always offer-ing something cool and exotic to try as well. They spend a great deal of time bringing in new products, staying with the times. As great as the place is, though, I have had constant issues with the cashiers/baggers. More than one seems to be untrained as to how to properly bag gro-ceries and interact with customers. More often than not, my nice peaches get squished by pints of ice cream that are carelessly thrown on top. This is only one example. I always have to talk to the baggers and walk them through how to properly package my goods, but the issue never seems to change. The cashiers ignore me and start ringing up the next person in line. While I am left to finish their bagging. At the point where the cashiers rolled their eyes at me because I had to point out that throwing tin cans on top of fresh tomatoes was not a good thing, I decided that they weren't willing to treat a customer, who supported a local independent business and continued to pay their higher prices to do so, with respect.

The worst of it is that the shopkeeper was always there. She has witnessed these exchanges, but never once did she step up and approach to acknowledge the issue. Instead, I was ignored. Worse still I felt iced out of my own community store as time went on (it was very clear to me that I was "that lady") simply for wanting basic customer service. Basic being the key word, because customer service is exactly that. In cases like this, it is so important for the manager to step up, own up, and address the situation. Not just for my sake but for the employees' sake too. What does this say to them? This, folks, is a perfect example of how *not* to get ahead of your competition. What really happened here is she allowed a bad situation. She was neither humble nor attentive, only annoyed. She was annoyed with me because I challenged her employees on how they were doing their jobs.

## DO YOUR BEST

In this vein, I urge your customer service people to always do their best. What do I mean by this? Have the right attitude.

## THE RIGHT ATTITUDE

What is the right kind of attitude to have when interacting with a customer? There is a certain attitude that is created by mixing equal parts "humility," "attentiveness," and "never being bothered." Use this formula. Remember, you are there for the customer above all. She doesn't want to know your problems or hear your excuses. Never make excuses for the bad things that happen around you, or the mistakes you make yourself. If a customer comments on the dirty bathroom in your shop, never say that it was because of your co-worker who had the shift before you, or you just don't know what goes on around here! This just brings negativity on your co-workers, your boss, and your company. Instead, apologize and tell the customer that you will fix it right away. Never make up excuses for yourself. All you have to do is address the concern and do the best that you can the next time.

Let the customer talk and you take notes. This method works especially well over the phone. Remember their dog's name, their birthdays, their vacations with their kids if that's what they love to regale you with, promotions, etc., etc. It is always very nice for them when you can refer back to it in further conversations.

Respond in a positive manner. Instead of answering, "No, we don't do that," which is full of negative words, answer, "That sounds really good, I'll check that out with my manager for you," as an example. There are specific ways that are appropriate to speak with customers. I like to tell my employees to use generally positive language that shows the customer they have pride in themselves and in the business. I prefer staff to be humble and kind, yet short in their responses. Double C and Double D, my language for Clear and Concise, Dignity and Decorum. Not too many customers want to hear your long-winded, muddled, or confusing story. So be quick and clear. Have respectful answers and never use any swear words.

### THE ABSOLUTE NO'S

We've gone through the important "do's" of customer service interactions, and now we will go through the absolute "don'ts" in customer service.

No personal phone. If you are on break and you want to be on your phone, exit any area where a customer can see you. You don't want a customer watching you twiddle with your phone while on break and assume you are goofing off while on shift.

This brings me to another "no," which is to make sure that there is no ambiguity about which staff member is working and which staff member is on break. Disney does a great job of upholding this rule at their theme parks. Many years ago, as I am sure it remains today, Disney ensured that all of their cast members remained out of sight when on break by creating a whole separate network of areas that their off-duty cast members could utilize. No child would come across Cinderella on her smoke break, or Mickey Mouse without his ears. When the characters were visible, they were always completely on, not stepping out of their roles. It is indicative of a strong business practice, but not necessarily something that you can reproduce in your business. Instead, you can make sure that your employees are out of uniform and/or out of sight. Have them take off their cap, badge, or any other accessory. Give them a break room to hang out in and keep their personal belongings as opposed to sitting directly beside the customers unless they are available to answer questions or help out.

Lastly, never ever speak negatively about your boss, co-workers, customers, or suppliers in front of or to customers. There are other outlets for this. If you have an issue, you should be going to your manager. Besides giving customers the idea that there is something wrong going on behind the scenes, it is one of the most unprofessional things you can do. The same goes for gossip. You aren't really paying attention to your customers at that point, now are you? I can't count how many times I've been in a store, looking around for assistance, and spotted two co-workers huddled in a corner gossiping while pretending to fold or sweep. Or suffered through the drama along with them at the cash register, even worse. I don't think that these employees are aware of the power of their actions. It speaks so poorly on the shopkeeper, and that is who ultimately suffers.

There is one topic of conversation that I am particularly against having between staff and that has to do with discussing salary and commissions. I beseech you to request that they not share information about their pay. I actually had to deal with an incident where a new employee did not fully understand her paycheck and stormed out to complain to the receptionist. In our front lobby! Of course, it is human nature to speak about private matters with friends and co-workers. I understand that, but please limit this type of information to a need-to-know basis, and tell your employees to do so as well. Let them know that if they have issues with their pay, then they should speak to their shopkeeper. If they don't want to do that, tell them to take it home to their dog.

All in all, I like to tell shopkeepers and employees to treat customers as if they were running a small business.

Regardless of your size, you should be offering personalized, feel-good service. Corporations bring to mind an industrial machine—a machine based on the bottom line, not the customer. One of the things that small and family-run businesses are best at is solving problems. They are able to address problems fast and efficiently. This is because they face issues head on. They have to. They have to be honest about their product or service, and deliver on their promise. When issues arise, customers know exactly where they can find a real person to speak to. Many successful large companies have adopted this philosophy and it works. Just listen to the automated message from Enterprise Car Rental while you're on hold, and you will know what I mean. They haven't failed yet to deliver on that promise, as I continue to use them when I travel.

When things go wrong in your business, as a shopkeeper just be humble, apologetic, and don't be averse to laughing at yourself. Everyone makes mistakes, or has a bad day, and humour is sometimes the best solution to any problem. For your customers, take care of the problem, make it right, and then apologize.

I have found that society has become more and more averse to the word "sorry" lately. When everything is subject to litigation, saying "sorry" is in fact admitting fault, so it seems. Others won't say sorry because they think it is weak. I disagree. It is part of allowing yourself to identify and fix a problem.

Whether there was any fault or not, by apologizing, you are telling the customer that you recognize that there is an issue and that you affirm their need at the moment. Once you do, then you can move on to fixing it. But you must take the time to recognize their frustration or even, sometimes, anger.

In my case, with the flight attendant I discussed at the very beginning of this book, I was completely ready to move on if he had simply recognized my frustration (and his own awkward behaviour) and subsequently apologized to me. There was no need to offer anything more than that or to rehash the situation. "I'm sorry" says it all and puts everyone back on track. And if you can't say "I'm sorry," then along the lines of "I understand" or "You've got it!" or "Let me fix this" will suffice.

### ON THE IMPORTANCE OF WRITING DOWN YOUR RULES

I've spoken a lot about the importance of communicating your rules to your employees. We've discussed that it is essential to be clear about the fundamentals during training and to reiterate them periodically even after training ends.

I want to go further with this and encourage you to write down your rules and make sure that your employees have access to them at all times. I like to turn mine into a poster and hang it in the break room. I want it to be very, very visible. This way, there is no ambiguity about what is expected of my employees. This is beneficial to the shopkeeper, because when the rules are displayed, it puts the onus on the employee to behave accordingly.

This practice is also helpful if an employee is constantly out of line and needs to be dealt with. The shopkeeper must follow the proper protocol when firing, but that employee will never have the excuse that he or she "didn't know the rules." At this point, he or she will have been trained properly and had access to the rules at all times. This helps to identify those bad employees who need to be picked out. If that employee is constantly doing things his or her way contrary to yours at his or her own discretion, bucking the system, and not respecting the clear rules, that person should be gone.

It is important to also make sure that each employee is clear as to why each rule exists. Take, for instance, the rule that states that employees should not wear open-toe shoes. If your employees complain about this, and are irritated that you are sabotaging their incredible fashion sense, all you need to do is explain why this is a rule. You must explain, that no, you are not trying to take away their independence, but rather, you are saving them from losing a toe. I guarantee they will understand rather quickly.

Now, you are the shopkeeper after all, and you shouldn't have to feel like you need to explain your rules if they are questioned too often. But you should be open to hearing complaints about them. By offering an ear, you help prevent your employees from going off and talking badly about it to each other. If there are suggestions from the staff about changes, be open. They will get on you, rightly so, if you answer their questions too often with, "Because I said so." That isn't really a reason. If someone brings up a good point about your rule in a roundtable discussion, it would beneficial to consider a change in accordance. Change is good because it means that you are innovating and moving forward. Enhance what works, but change what doesn't. Some rules or practices become outdated, and so you must be able to change with the times. Call it the Baked Ham Moment.

I like to think of this as similar to the experiment with mice. Scientists created a maze and placed a piece of food at the end. They set the mice loose in the maze to find the food. Over and over again, the scientists executed the same experiment, with the food always in the same place. Then, one day, they changed the location of the food. They watched as some mice took the same route that they had been taking, over and over. Other mice, however, were able to change their practices to find the new location of the food. These mice survived.

This is a perfect allegory for the need to adjust to the times, to changing conditions, to anticipated bumps in the road, and to becoming too complacent.

Next I offer two comprehensive examples of how I think the rules should be written out. Feel free to borrow some of the points for your posters!

### BIG JOHN'S FOOTWEAR FOR MEN

A warehouse distributor for all-weather work boots and outdoor footwear that sells to various type of stores and buys large quantities and overstocked items from manufacturers.

### TO ALL EMPLOYEES
Code of Conduct:

- Remember we are all here to sell shoes, not to find out who won on *The Bachelorette*.
- We do not fraternize; we like everyone we hire and want to keep them.
- Please check the expiry date on your deodorant for all our sake's.

- We will discuss any issues or concerns in private.
- No cussing. Period.
- Lunch is to be enjoyed in the lunchroom only.
- Your mom isn't coming in after to clean it up for you.
- All coffee mugs used by you will be washed by you at the end of the day *with soap*.
- Please find the fan switch in the bathroom.

On the Job:

- All customers deserve the same respect regardless of how big the order or question.
- There is never a stupid question.
- Trying your best gets noticed, so does going above and beyond your job.
- Always follow-up with a phone call after an order has been shipped.
- Admitting a mistake and seeking assistance will help save your job; hiding it won't.
- Our shipments don't go out because someone took an order; it is everyone's responsibility to see it through with quality and timeliness.
- The phone is always answered, and a call is always transferred to someone who is present and on duty.
- We like it when you have ideas you would like to share.

- Three- or four-hour shifts: You may be called in to cover a shift or asked to work longer hours.
- Wait staff: Taking orders/bringing orders to kitchen, serving food and drinks, keeping all areas clean, making coffees, answering phone, food prep, bake, work cash register. Management will direct you to the appropriate station.
- Remember, no job is too great or too small for any of us.
- If not busy, ask where you can help. There is always something to be done.
- Get familiar with every aspect of the workplace. Be very knowledgeable about the food, drinks, baking, products, order-taking, etc., and our business philosophy.
- Be able (with confidence) to answer customers' questions. If you are not sure just ask. We are here to help you perform your job to the best of your ability.
- *Always* be polite and respectful to customers as well as co-workers. Be professional. Be gracious.

Rules and Regulations:

- Always keep busy and helpful.
- Always look presentable, neat, and tidy, and wear the proper uniform. If you come to work otherwise dressed, you may be asked to go home and change.
- Wear proper footwear, comfortable and practical—no

open toes.

- Do not be late. If you know you are running late, you must call in to let us know. We will expect you to make up the time at the end of your shift.
- Breaks will be taken in designated locations only and absent of any apron or name tags.
- No employee is allowed behind the bar, in the back room, or kitchen when not on shift. No customers are allowed in those areas.
- Be ready to start your shift at it's start time. Don't walk in right at start time.
- If you need a day off when you would otherwise be scheduled, please submit a note a minimum of two weeks prior or before next schedule is written.

Absolutely NO:

- NO inappropriate language.
- NO personal talk in front of customers. Leave personal issues at home; keep work conversation neutral.
- NO negative comments about other staff, owner, food, pay cheques, hours, etc., while on the floor. Set up a time with management/owner to discuss in private.
- NO cell phones on your person or near you or being used while on your shift.

Note: We take the above points very seriously, there will be *zero* tolerance.

WORK AS A TEAM! BE POSITIVE! ENJOY THE JOB! TAKE PRIDE AND FEEL GOOD ABOUT MAKING SOMEONE'S DREAM COME TRUE! And for goodness' sake, HAVE FUN! We want this to succeed for all of us.

In the space provided, write about how you would alter these lists, or how you would write one of your own in a different type of industry. You may also use this to add what you feel are important aspects specific to you.

_____

_____

_____

_____

_____

Next, I discuss tips for using this practice in real-life situations. Here we will address all of the needs of the customer that you should be aware of successfully satisfying.

You must be mindful of addressing the needs of your customers in all ways. *What* you do is just as important as *how* you do it. The world is evolving to become a more mindful place, and you must evolve with it. Therefore, you must be more ethically, environmentally, and culturally aware. Millennials get this. They have been taught to look at the long term, to care about the planet as well as the people who are on it. This means that you, as a shopkeeper, must be wary that your products and practices reflect this. Keep packaging simple, green, and clean. Packaging waste and other excess waste is looked down upon. Additionally, make sure that your workspace is clean and functioning. There is no such thing as "it's not my job" when it comes to cleanliness.

You must also reflect this ideology in the way that you speak to your customers. Millennials are extraordinarily aware that using appropriate and inclusive language is very important in this day and age. You can barely go a week without hearing about a company getting slayed on the Internet and in the mainstream media over a story of an offended customer. Please make sure to properly address people as "Ms." or "Mr." Don't simply assume; don't make the mistake of reading your customers improperly. Case in point: Why am I constantly addressed as "Mrs." when I am on my own, never mind that plenty of women prefer Ms. Is it because of my age? Would that make single women my age feel uncomfortable if they were always addressed that way? Aren't there plenty of women who are married who prefer Ms.? You don't know, so accept the importance of what it means to not know.

You must keep in mind, too, the different types of customers that you will need to accommodate. You must always consider the nutritional and dietary confinements of your customers. Thirty years ago, most people didn't even know what a vegan was. Today, there are numerous dietary and allergy restrictions that you have to be able to work with.

Today, people have very strong reactions to what you offer and how you offer it. I think that this is a great step forward as we move into a future where everyone is respected.

This leads into my next point: treat all customers the same. Why wouldn't you? You must respect your customer regardless of age, gender, language, nationality, or race.

Never ignore or give lesser service to a group of young people. I treated my two kids and myself to a vacation last summer through a company that prides itself on its impeccable customer service. This was no ordinary trip; it was a multi-week tour, and I also like to bring my kids with me because they are wonderful people whom I have a lot of fun with. They are respectful, considerate young adults who get along famously with an older crowd, and so we had a fabulous time, save for a couple of incidents.

The incidents occurred because one particular crew member, who acted as the "head" concierge for all of the guests, could not hide her animosity towards the fact that my children were on the trip. The trip was expensive, and it was mostly populated by older, retired couples. Note that my children were nineteen and twenty, so they are not really children anymore. A great many of the other guests got along splendidly with them and joked about how my kids were so incredibly lucky to be on this trip, and they weren't wrong! It was clear that this particular woman was treating them differently—my kids who had paid the same as everyone else is how I like to put it. The woman never once addressed them on her own accord throughout the twenty-four day excursion. The only time she ever spoke to them was when another adult was with them. Her job was to ask about and see to what the guests needed, but never once did she offer her services to my children. Not only that, but on multiple occasions, they both found her pointedly making them feel uncomfortable and not welcome with her sour stares. Her mistake was not acknowledging the paying, respectful customers that they were. I didn't find her particularly nice to her staff either. This was a case where we were very happy to fill out the questionnaire at the end. The company, a leader in customer service in their industry, reacted accordingly. There should never be any reason to look at people differently, as they are buying your product or service, unless under exceptionally difficult circumstances of course. Be able to identify and use your discretion when dealing with situations that are harmful or toxic to your environment.

Never underestimate the power of the people you are serving.

Do not patronize those who do not speak your native tongue. If someone is a foreigner and not a regular customer, treat that person the same whether you think he or she will return or not.

If your customer does not appear to be in the demographic that you are targeting, that shouldn't matter. You should have the same respect and approach the situation with the same dignity that you provide everyone else.

Remember, everyone's money is the same colour. It's an old expression, but it is timeless.

The Millennials get this; they really do. They're a part of a generation that is already more inclusive and accepting than any generation before them. I still find my children asking me how on earth my generation (and my parents' generation) allowed certain terrible things to be said or done. You don't have to tell them and their peers that the way some things used to be was wrong; they already know it, but you still have to convince some people my age of that fact.

This leads me to another issue that I have with businesses that offer special deals or memberships to specific groups of people. It's my opinion that businesses should give all of their customers the best price that they can for the product or service offered. If pricing is true, then shopkeepers shouldn't feel the need to give specials or discounts. There are other, more creative, ways to offer rewards to loyalty. The same company from the trip tour story earlier, a luxury worldwide hotel to be precise, certainly recognized how much I did and have spent within their whole organization and subsequently gave me access to a personal concierge that I only have to contact and all my requests will be taken care of no matter where and how I use their services. It's a new service they are presenting, as they too continue to work to improve with the times, as I will be mentioning a little later on. Most importantly, it is handled privately, not in front of any other customers.

When you treat all your customers with the same respect, they will respect you back. And they will show respect to you by giving you positive feedback. Nowadays, with the Internet and the use of phone apps that allow crowdsourcing information and opinions, many businesses live and die by their customer reviews. Your reviews on Yelp and similar sites truly make a difference.

Yes, absolutely, some customers will be mean, rude, and

nasty—but, that is the nature of the beast. Prepare yourself and your staff to deal with it.

# CHAPTER
# FOUR

. . . . . . . . . . . . . . . . . . . . . . . . . . . .

# MANY DANCES, SIMILAR STEPS

. . . . . . . . . . . . . . . . . . . . . . . . . . . .

## CUSTOMER SERVICE ACROSS INDUSTRIES

n this chapter, we will outline the similarities and differences in customer service across industries and in businesses both big and small.

## IS CUSTOMER SERVICE THE SAME ACROSS ALL INDUSTRIES?

First, I want to reiterate that all prior discussion in this book applies to *all* businesses, regardless of industry. Our discussions are widely applicable because they speak to the inherent rules of operating a viable business. Second, all businesses must consider and/or battle against failure. All businesses are selling a product, or a service. If they don't sell, they are done. It doesn't matter if you are selling $1 slices of pizza out of a pushcart on a corner or if you are selling $20,000 handbags on Fifth Avenue, if you move furniture for people or if you are a real estate developer. All businesses *will* fail if the product or service doesn't sell. Third, every person in any business has a role in the ultimate success of that business. The salesperson, the designer, the advertiser, IT, the warehouse person, the team leader, they all have a role to properly fulfill and must be respected as such. The dance is dependent upon the involvement of all parties.

## HOW IS CUSTOMER SERVICE DIFFERENT ACROSS ALL INDUSTRIES?

The fundamentals of customer service are the same across all industries; however, there are variables that should factor into the minutia of how customer service ultimately applies to your specific business.

The fundamental structure and offerings of your business necessitate a specific type of customer service. I am speaking to the basics of your business; the products or services your business offers. The following industries all demand a particular type of approach to customer service: hospitality and tourism; cable, communication, and tech; financial; car sales and real estate; transportation; industrial; retail; home services; medical and research; and entertainment including sports and amusement, parks and concerts are excellent examples. All of these industries offer different services, experiences, and products and thus all need a specific type of customer service model and culture based on the demographic(s) they are selling to.

In order to understand what I mean about specialized customer service rules, let's analyze the particulars of the sports and entertainment industry. The amount of work that goes into any sporting event should astound you. Sporting events by nature are massive, costly, and require an incredibly intricate dance between customer and customer service representative. The sheer amount of people attending these events demands a specific type of customer service representative. Specifically, one that can stay organized and move large amounts of (let's say it: prone to be intoxicated) people in and out safely and efficiently. This type of customer service person will most likely be loud, resistant to bullshit, and fast-paced. If you think that this service rep would bode well selling high-end dresses in Manhattan, you would be severely mistaken.

I have found that American companies that put on these grand events housing tens of thousands are truly on task. They have no choice in the highly competitive world that is theirs. Someone else *will* gladly take that contract. American companies appear to be very conscious of providing the correct number of entrances, toilets, food stations, parking spaces, and easily identifiable help. They execute so well because they make sure to provide an adequate number of staff. In comparison, cities such as Toronto get away with too little staff. More often than not, they are only just gruff or appear aloof. And if you want a slice of pizza or a hot dog at an event, sadly there is not usually very much choice, you better be willing to stand in line for a while. When my family and I go to games, we draw straws for who has to do it. And don't even talk to me about what it's like leaving an outdoor concert through the only narrow avenue out! Anyone with claustrophobia, beware.

It is clear to me, during these times, just how much better we deserve to be treated.

## CUSTOMER SERVICE IN ONLINE BUSINESSES

It is also crucial to include an assessment of customer service with respect to online businesses. After all, these businesses are increasing in their percentage of the future. On the surface, it would appear they are primarily "do it yourself" businesses. The customer is mostly servicing himself and interacting with an algorithm. Therefore, you must be wondering, "Why do we need to talk about customer service for online businesses?" This is not a silly question, by all means. I had an interaction with a small lovely group of entrepreneurs, intelligent and professional in their particular field, who did not actually have customer service addressed as a role. They do now. We need to discuss it because there are important facets of customer service at play behind the scenes.

First, you must consider who the people are who initially attract customers to that specific online business. Competition for online market share is fierce, and so you must reflect on the type of customer service person who can capture customers' attention. Online businesses must hire online architects who cater specifically to drawing in a crowd. They must consider the appropriate content, design, and message that is displayed on the site. They must make sure to make the site simple and navigable so that customers are led to purchasing and can get all the help that they need in the process. Not to mention for follow-up!

Businesses that offer most, if not all of their services through the web, must make sure that the process is not just in plain language but thorough enough so customers don't have to call in or find a store. This defeats the whole purpose of leading the customer to purchase online in the first place! You want your customers to be able to get as much out of the experience as possible. If your online platform can't bring them that, and if you can't answer their questions via online chat, then you should rethink your platform if that's your direction. Not to mention, in case you somehow missed it, this has become an excellent, uber-efficient way of capturing a wealth of information on client profiles—personal info regarding ways to contact them and experience/opinion gathering, which is free as long as you can get them to complete the transaction.

For example, I was at a point where I needed to install Internet at a place I keep in the South. Awesome job this particular company did inviting me to do it all online. I couldn't get to what I needed, however, simply because I was from a different country, and so five minutes in, I already was forced to pick up the phone. I called in, spoke to a machine, and pressed a countless number of buttons trying to navigate to a real voice. They really wanted me to do this online. But there was no option for me. Finally, I was told that I had two problems, both stemming from the fact that I wasn't a resident.

Fortunately, for me, the story takes a dramatic turn here. And, despite the frustration I felt with their online and tele-services, I ultimately left happy.

I walked into one of their stores, and immediately I was approached by a young woman who asked me what I needed. I told her my predicament, but assured her that I was willing to pay a fee or anything else that she needed in order to give me Internet. Perhaps my first born? Can you imagine how I am feeling at this point, believing I may not be able to have it? Let *that* sink in. This had to happen and what I was truly hoping for was true customer service: someone who was dedicated to finding a solution and wouldn't leave me until we had. I had two teenagers. Enough said.

The manager said, "Yes, ma'am, we will figure this all out." She handed me over to Myron, one of her employees, and he assured me, although appearing a tad nervous, that we would make this happen. I appreciated him admitting to me that he didn't actually know all the answers, but that we would work together to figure it all out. Myron was exceedingly patient with me as we did just that and began the process of filling out paperwork. We set up details, including automatic payment, and filled out a ton of paperwork.

Still, we went through more steps, and Myron was starting to sweat. It had become pretty complicated, but, again, he assured me that he would see this through. He did. Then we hit a roadblock on the final step on his handy little iPad that he was working through in an attempt to pay the service fee. It was my Visa. When attempting to verify the postal code, the entry line wouldn't accept it. We could not change it, so we called a central office, but they didn't have an answer for us. The manager in the store took note of this glitch and assured me that she would follow-up to see that it was taken care of. The "glitch," which I identified, was that the line the form provided only allowed five spaces, as all American postal codes contain. Not so with mine, which requires six and contains both alphabetic and numeric figures.

Finally, it was realized that one of the options was to just pay cash. Myron took it and handed me a receipt. By this point, we were both practically shedding tears of joy—he as much as I. I thanked Myron for putting up with me for so long. I even joked about how he knew now what my kids went through every day, and he laughed.

Yes, Myron saved the day for me, but I chose to share so much of this story because I could not believe what had happened in the end. This is a very large tele and Internet company, but what happened with their online platform? Where was the disconnect? The genius tech person (and believe me, this got by more than one person) that pulled it all together had made a mistake. He or she had failed to think about the people who were paying with credit cards who were based outside of the country. One small, tiny, yet oh so crucial, element. This is such an important thing to consider. Our world is a global one; you must make sure that you can cater to it. Nowadays, we have a fluid world, and many people who move within it. Dialling it down even further, that city has an incredible university that accepts foreign students not necessarily arriving with "local" credit cards but ones from their home countries. Something to think about.

### CUSTOMER SERVICE AND BUSINESS SIZE
Differences in Customer Service Based on Company Size

Customer service differs depending on company size. Essentially, the size of your business can dictate *what* you deliver and *how* you deliver it. Bigger companies deal with larger volumes of product and longer distances to deliver that product. This means that there is a greater potential to run into logistical setbacks. Bigger companies also must cater to a larger customer base. In order to do this, bigger companies must house more employees. They are also inherently held to a higher standard of service. For that reason, staff must be expertly trained and thoroughly knowledgeable.

Small businesses have a shorter distance between shopkeeper and customer. This alters the relationship between them in a fundamental way. There are more face-to-face, human-to-human interactions. Because of this, the way in which you deliver the promise to the customer is different. For instance, the customer demands more access to the shopkeeper of a smaller business. And when they don't have it, you will surely hear about it.

Differently sized companies must deal with competition differently. Larger companies, by default, likely deal with an enormous amount of competition. For example, smaller companies do everything in their power to take a percentage away from these larger businesses. Likewise, direct competitors do so as well. If your larger business is unable to withstand this barrage, then you will have to change your practices. Sometimes that means constantly seeking new and innovative ways to continue.

Again, consistently monitor your business. I bring you back again to the airline attendant. Make sure that you are implementing or exercising ways to stand back and capture how your business is running. Be your own customer. Ask your employees what is going on. Address issues head on.

I was travelling for business and had a two-day layover in New York. I was shopping in a relatively small chain store and saw a pair of boots that my daughter would have loved. The store didn't have her size, but the salesperson assured me that they would have her proper size ready for me to pick up the next morning on my way out to the airport. I was assured over and over by the salesperson that they would have the boots for me at 10:00 a.m., and he took my cell number. Of course, I was to pay for them first. So I arrived the next morning to pick up the boots, and upon my entrance into the store, the staff scattered. I was short on time and couldn't spare a moment for that nonsense, so I chased one of the salespeople down. She told me that a girl named Katie would "handle me," and then she jetted off into the back of the store.

I was not entirely sure who Katie was, but I *was* entirely sure that something had gone wrong with my order.

Katie eventually came out from the back and introduced herself to me as the manager of the store and explained they didn't have the boots for me. The pair had come in last evening from another location nearby but it was discovered then that the box contained two different sized boots. What is the most important mistake here? No one called me as soon as they realized the problem. What is the next step for the manager, and was she not monitoring well enough to be aware herself? How she handled this next was a crucial moment for a small business. A large company would have simply credited me; of course, they also may have been less likely to have been put in that situation in the first place, but my moment was saved when she offered to either credit me or overnight a new pair from a different location direct to me at my destination in LA. Preferably, she looked for ways afterwards to train her staff on handling the issue better than they had upon my return to the store. "Scatter," indeed.

### Similarities in Customer Service Regardless of Company Size

Although it seems as though it is far easier for a shop-keeper to monitor his staff when operating within a small business, this is patently untrue. A large corporation can (and is required to) monitor its staff just as effectively. This can be done if the corporation has an appropriate number of staff and an empowered middle or upper management that is not afraid to make decisions or, sometimes, take risks.

The example of my experience with the Internet provider proves this point. I was given exceptional service. Myron, the salesman who helped me, ended our interaction by giving me his card and his cell phone number, explaining that he cared enough to want to know my installation went well and as scheduled. Furthermore, he made sure to call to check in to see if the technician showed up and followed up again at a later date, checking that my service and package were complete. During these exchanges, kept short and succinct, I kept thinking how I would have hired him in a second at my company. He was dedicated to his job, knew of his avenues for support, was a firecracker, and had the confidence and wherewithal to follow-up with monitoring his co-worker, product, and service. And he was a junior.

Focusing on forward movement, innovation, and changing with the times is also an arena that is shared. All companies, regardless of size, need to stay on top of what customers want. This is because innovation and movement happens when companies listen to what their customers want and need. Ask your customers what they are lacking and what they are wanting. Have you talked to your customers personally? What are they telling you? What do you yourself see? What's in the future? What's coming down the pipe, and how can you react to it now? All companies need to be looking to the outside world in order to understand where the needs of their customers are likely heading. Where is your room for growth and other areas that you can add to enhance your product or service? Look at what feels like the natural progression of it and react to it when and if you are able.

All companies, regardless of size, must also set goals. Shopkeepers must keep customers, maximize profits, stay on top of customers' essential needs, and deliver on the promise. They also need to attract customers to make sales in order to survive. This is the law of business.

Let's recall the story about the employees at the Toronto Airport security line. How do these two employees deliver on the promise of travel management?

_____

_____

_____

_____

_____

Answer: They are delivering on the promise of travel-time management by providing great customer service when time is of the essence. They are always showing the customer that they care about destinations being reached at a time when it's needed most.

It is one thing for a business to make a promise regarding a product or service, but it is also a very important thing for that business to materialize that promise into physical signage. Investing in beautifully branded signage that exclaims your promise is encouraged. Anything extra that you can materialize that directs your promise to your customers is also beneficial. My city's airport, since we are already on this topic, has developed well-crafted signs that attract attention. Specifically, their signs that say, "Please report to security if you notice anything suspicious," are placed in proper locations throughout the facility. These signs appear in a way that tell their customers that they should always feel comfortable, not silly or afraid. But most important is how they follow through; easily identifiable "security" is apparent and available without having to hunt it down. Something that you are not likely to do as you are working on getting to those lovely security people as soon as possible. The airport is visually delivering on its promise of safe and efficient air travel.

I encountered something very suspicious in the parking garage on my way to a flight. As I walked into the airport, I debated on whether I should tell anyone what I saw. I was just about to convince myself it was probably nothing and

I didn't have time when I saw their clear sign. It reminded me that it was OK to feel suspicious, and it took me less than five seconds to spot security personnel. I reported the incident and felt better about it afterward.

This dance, this offering of great customer service regardless of the size of your business takes time. Therefore, you must be patient. If you work toward a goal with good intentions, your environment will only get better. A dance looks great on stage, but the audience never sees all of the quality work that went on behind the scenes. This behind-the-scenes work is where progress is made and where bugs are worked out.

### KEY TIPS TO ELEVATE CUSTOMER SERVICE INTERACTION

What are some tips for any business, large or small, in any industry to use in order to elevate their customer service interaction?

Vary the dynamics of the customer service staff. Differences in your staff allow everyone to bring something unique to the table. At this intersection of diverse minds, you can tap into a mix of ideas, experiences, and opinions. Don't be afraid of this! It is amazing how people with different styles and personalities can get along really well. They will learn from each other, and we all must be constantly learning in order to grow and develop.

Don't limit your staff to a certain age or gender. This is an old-school, outdated practice. Utilize staff with different language backgrounds, styles, and personality types. People are so different from each other (think in terms of both customers *and* staff), so embrace that and use it to your advantage. I think customers respond to diversity. If your customer can identify in some way with a particular person on your staff, then they will feel as if they are being included in a special way.

I've had experiences where I've seen a group of three same-age teenage girls working together. They were unable to get along because they all wanted to be the lead, yet none had experience and maturity, and they were always competing. I've experienced in the past a group of all middle-aged men with the same background and set in their ways, where innovation was slowed or halted altogether.

All companies should watch what works and move people as necessary.

Companies should know their competition and work to determine why and how they can be better. Every employee in a company should be thinking about this.

Know the industry. If there is a gap, be ready to fill it. Back in the '70s, an ad campaign ran that took charge of a gap in the soda industry that Coke, Pepsi, and others had left open. The company launched 7 Up, as the "Uncola," complete with a visual image of the Uncola Nut: a half lemon, half lime creation. The simplicity was as great as its effectiveness. We liked to say back then that the person who came up with it was sitting on a porch somewhere with his feet up smoking a big cigar. I use that expression today when talking about a great achievement.

Listen to what people are talking about to find that gap. You don't necessarily have to invent a whole new product. You can rework an old product or service: deliver it in a new way, package it in a novel fashion, or market it in a new light.

Lastly, remember that, some day, the dance will inevitably change, and you will need to be ready to learn new steps.

# CHAPTER
# FIVE

. . . . . . . . . . . . . . . . . . . . . . . . . . . . . .

# KEEPING DANCING

. . . . . . . . . . . . . . . . . . . . . . . . . . . . . .

## F/U STANDS FOR
## FOLLOW UP

o you know what the opposite of love is? Would you say that it is hate? Most people would say yes, but the opposite of love is actually indifference.

Indifference is not caring one way or another.

Do you know what the worst feeling that you can give a customer is? The worst feeling isn't sad, nor disappointed, nor angry. Because that would mean there was at least an exchange. The worst feeling you can give a customer is one of being invisible.

In order to prevent this feeling of invisibility, it is important to first acknowledge a customer's presence. If you are swamped, make eye contact and smile or nod at him or her until you can make time to interact with that person. This is an incredible moment of attention that is too often disregarded, yet means so much to the customer. The same goes for over the phone. You can acknowledge by calling to let the customer know you are aware of them and will be in touch as soon as possible (for example, "Ted passed on your request and I will be looking after you..."). Continue that attentiveness to your customer at all points of your interaction, even after the sale is over. Then continue to evaluate what your customer needs, listen to your customer, and labor to adapt and to practice flexibility.

What do I mean by evaluate your customer's needs even after the sale? You must anticipate his needs and give him the experience that he was promised. Even after the sale, you should still listen to the customer. Be open to conversation and to complaints, even nonsensical ones. Sometimes all you have to say to your customer is "I understand" or "Yes, Sir." Customers like to rant and talk in circles because, as a customer service rep, you are basically a captive audience. People feel better after letting off steam, so simply nod, try to understand, and offer help if any. It will go a long way. And remember, you may not be able to please everyone but you can sure try.

After the sale is finished, do not lose all sense of professionalism. Continue to refrain from negative, derogatory, or inappropriate language. If customers are ranting in a negative way, don't commiserate with them. There is a way to listen to your customer and sympathize without contributing. If, for instance, a customer is complaining about the service at another company, don't say, "Yeah,

I know. They suck!" Instead, say something like "Wow, I had no idea. I really don't know why that would be!"

Your job in customer service has not ended when the product has shipped or the service call is over or when there is only a one-time purchase. Preferably, there is a time and situation allowance for ensuring the end result was satisfactory. In conversations post-sale, sometimes you will get very positive comments from the customer about his or her experience. It feels good to get positive feedback from customers, so for goodness' sake, spread that compliment throughout the staff! Positive comments inevitably reinvigorate the dance, and so the whole team benefits. It's nice to be reminded about why you do your job in the first place.

Keep dancing after the sale: Follow-up with your customer in order to assure that he never feels invisible. Even if you have the type of business where your only future contact is a repeat visit physically. The dance never stops.

We came up on the two-year anniversary of our café in February of 2016. We had gained a reputation as an inviting, homey yet classy café that never compromised on quality and nary an empty table. We had managed to maintain this reputation through the beginning years, which, for any restaurant, are notoriously rocky.

We built our reputation organically by word of mouth and consistently great service and products. Every customer was treated well. People loved and continue to love us. For instance, there is an older gentleman who comes into our café four times a week. This is amazing because we are only open five days a week! He sat down at our bar one day and said, "You know, I just lost the last two people in my life. My mother and my best friend are gone. I don't have very many people in my life, and it's a sad time for me right now. That's why I come here, because you make me feel like family."

It was the best compliment I could ever imagine. It didn't get much better than that for us. It's the stuff that makes the long hard hours, the trials and tribulations, so very worth it.

We have little old ladies that come for tea and pastries at three o'clock. We have office workers in at the lunch rush. We have real estate agents and lawyers come in for their power talks. We have an old boys club that takes their coffee at the same corner table every morning for a couple hours. We have retirees who come to read the paper. Our café has become a ritual for all of them.

You can often hear the kitchen call out our motto, "Made with love!" when food comes out. That is our saying because we want to keep the promise of food made with love. We want that promise to stick with our customers even after they walk out of the door. But all of this did not happen simply because we wanted it to.

Despite all of this positivity, we don't pretend to know exactly what our customers want and need. We don't get cocky, and so we make sure to stay on top of things; we are always following up with our customers to see how we can continue or adapt to meet their needs. We listen and evaluate in order to expand upon what works and what doesn't work. We keep moving forward and change when things aren't working, and sometimes we even change when things *are* working.

This piece of advice seems kind of counter-intuitive; why would you change things that are working well? Sometimes, changes are simply necessary.

At that two-year anniversary, it was decided that we needed a change, despite the fact that things were running smoothly. It was not so much about altering the fundamental characteristics of our café that made it such a magnetic place, but implementing changes for future growth in sales. Namely, I wanted to pivot so that we could offer more to our customers. We needed an upgrade, so I sat down with my partner and my team and asked them what they thought was really working.

Across the board, everyone agreed that the salads that we offered were really, *really* working. Our salads are beyond fresh, always change, and are very well put together. They are enhanced with dressing from our own personal repertoire and customers can't get enough of it! At their request, we started offering dressing in jars they can buy to take home. I also have a special, natural method for cleaning lettuce that makes my salads superior. Sounds like a little thing to gush over, but this *is* what our customers want. Not just the customers but the staff as well all say that they won't eat salads anywhere else! So why would we change that? We didn't change it; we expanded upon it.

We tried two new things. We implemented a "build your own salad" and, as an addendum, we added a "build your own sandwich." This was not the typical four different salads to choose from, and three different proteins that they could add. This was a well-planned list (that needed slight modification as we learned over time) of a variety of twenty-plus items that gave the customer the ability to literally design it themselves, with enough additional proteins to satisfy all dietary requirements, including those with allergies, fresh made to order. We gave them a card to fill out, even with sizing options, and they loved the concept. Again, we were more *personal*. Not one size fits all. It was rather quite interesting, some of the creations that went out, but they were getting exactly what they wanted. The sandwich idea eventually needed to be removed, but the "build your own salad" was an absolute blowout hit. We eventually added more seating outside and many came before the start of lunch service to be assured of a table. For us it wasn't about generating more work—we were already very busy making our wonderful salads—it was about listening and creating imaginatively and setting ourselves ahead of the competition. We often hear regulars, as they bring new people in to try us out, say, "You won't get a better salad than here."

We had to alter a few things to get the concept right. We were asking questions and listening to the customers but also to the front and kitchen staff. This was follow-up. We found that our cards needed layout adjustments in order for the kitchen to keep up with the new demand. Our customers also asked for additional items to choose from.

In the end, this new idea worked well for us. It is an important lesson for the shopkeeper as well as staff; even though sales were on target, we still needed to communicate with customers, continue to build on our success, keep our ideas fresh, and follow through.

· · ·

To conclude, I'd like to speak to some questions and concerns about customer service that come up frequently.

**1.** *How do we get our promise to stick with our customers as they walk out of our doors?*

Through great branding that remains in their heads until long after they've purchased.

Branding is the wave of the future. Branding is where companies are allocating a lot of resources today because it is the medium in which the signature of the company is manifested. Branding today is different from what it was twenty years ago. It has grown massively in the wake of the Millennial generation. One of the reasons for this, I believe, is because the Millennial generation understands the importance of, and is quasi-obsessed with, it. You can see it even in the way that Millennials brand *themselves.* They literally wear who they are. They express their individuality by branding themselves through unique clothing, hairstyles, and body modifications, in particular with tattoos that are given quite a bit of thought.

Millennials are also heavily focused on branding in the businesses that they operate. I believe that they are able to understand the importance of it because they are more in touch with their innate creative abilities. Millennials have been taught that there is a creative instinct in everyone; Millennials are exploring themselves as artists, musicians, writers, and photographers and so are constantly expressing this creativity. They know that everyone has the ability to tap into this ingenuity to further their career, business, family, and life. The Millennial generation understands this and has capitalized on it.

You can leverage customer service in order to support your company's specific and unique brand. Customer service allows you to translate your memorable signature onto the customer. Your staff is there to deliver that promise. Your brand is your promise. They must be consistent in delivering that promise and that brand.

## 2. *How do you find that memorable signature?*

First, look for what is missing. Do you feel there is a hole in the market? Is what you offer able to fill a gap in a product or service? Is there a better way to deliver or service, or how would *you* like it to look or be done? Can you offer something more? When you ask yourself these questions, don't just look internally, make sure to be thorough and reflect upon and discover what the world is missing. Oftentimes, we think, "Oh, I wish there was this type of service" or, "It should be done this way." Keep notes, especially about your own dreams and what you feel the future may hold.

There is a thriving business in my home town, a fairly new

privately owned company, offering lawn care and design landscaping. Even the name, Lawn Troopers, seemed to fit well. I watched the young man who started it work very long and hard establishing himself, exemplary really, with a staff that was clearly trained in providing professionalism and respectfulness to their clients and came with a variety of backgrounds, experiences, and ages. I do believe he won an Entrepreneur of the Year Award early on. I met up with him recently and, in conversation, learned that he has since added a host of other services—things that would certainly enhance or "marry" with what he already provided. These were not necessarily the "norm" for this type of business, but great ideas to expand his business on. Clearly a lot of thought, planning and organizing had gone into it.

On another note, there are extra habits you can adopt that put you ahead of where your competition likely stays. For one, there is staying power, afforded by you personally. If I had to name one particular thing that stood out in my early years of developing my own customer service personality, it was that I never went home when there was a crisis at my customer's end. I never left a panicked buyer, an engineer, or QC person without doing everything I could to help or support *regardless* of whether the issue was over at my end or not. I saw it through with them. Don't go home until your customer or client does.

They don't forget that. When your customer pays for your service, his biggest value comes from what else you can do for them. These are things that will put you in that elite category you just may be looking for.

**3.** *How do you manage to think about the future, especially when it seems impossible to imagine?*

Early in my career in wire and cable distribution, we were at the cusp of the wireless telecommunications revolution. At that point, we didn't entirely know what was yet to come, but saw the companies we were working with gearing up for it.

We had started with those gigantic car phones that plugged into cigarette lighters. It was, for lack of better words, a huge box. The antennae was long, and the phone itself was bulky. It was a great day when we moved up in the world with the flip up cellular phones.

I was in that room one day with some pretty important players in the industry when someone said where this was all going. We were told that sometime in the future everyone would be designated with their own personal singular phone number and, with that, would be reachable wherever they were in the world. It was incredible to us how that was possible. But at that moment, even though we had a lot to learn (and to do) we realized that we were looking at the very future. When Blackberry announced the capability to email anyone from your phone, it was revolutionary. It changed the face of conducting business.

Don't be afraid to explore the future to find your memorable signature. There is nothing wrong with looking back, but don't dwell on the past. Allow your company to stand out from the crowd and move forward and show your incredible ideas, your pool of talent, and your energy.

4. *How can companies stay a step ahead of changes?*

To continue the discussion from earlier about maintaining a grasp on future trends, let's explore how, exactly, you can accomplish this seemingly impossible task. I think that the best way to answer this question is through an anecdote.

The Four Seasons is a company that prides itself on being a luxury hotel chain that is focused, first and foremost, on their customers. Elite men and women from all over the globe call upon the Four Seasons when they are looking for an especially dignified personally attentive service-oriented experience.

When I travel, I stay at the Four Seasons. I have been doing so for many, many years. From their then humble beginnings, they have touted the impeccable service they chose to offer, but also maintained their professional courtesy in affording privacy to their guests and a familiar stay for the famous. It is their calling tag and a substantial part of how they branded themselves.

The hotels themselves are designed elegantly and simplistically. To me it is a classy, old-school experience. But times are changing. Companies are now injecting personality, humour, and excitement into their brands. Creativity reigns now and brands are expected to have a specific voice. Take excellent ones such as Virgin Airlines who are pushing the limits. They are a great example of a company that has adopted branding that can be creative, erotically sentient, and exciting. Our culture has undergone a paradigm shift; experiences must now be more colourful and stimulating. Media must grab viewers and speak to them in the new way of absorbing and enticing. Just look at the way cinematographers have changed the way we view things in the last five years. The way it moves, the rhythm, is spectacularly different. They are the rock stars.

Let's look again at the Four Seasons in terms of the Millennials being their future. It is time for a freshening, time to adapt to this changing world in a more vibrant way. They are, in fact, creating new advertisements through more exciting promotional videos as well as new opportunities that include journeys taking their level of service into other areas, such as their group private jet experience. Which, by the way, is attended by as diverse of a clientele as the world now beholds, and their marketing should be proud to reflect this. It would serve them well not to miss that boat, or in this case jet.

**5.** *Why is it important not to stand on your competitors' failures?*

Don't waste time or energy complaining about your competitors to your clients. This advice is pertinent for more reasons than you might think. By highlighting your competition to your customers (even in a negative light), you are offering information about them. Even bad attention is attention. Every minute you are talking negatively about your competition, you are missing an opportunity to talk positively about yourself. Always take every opportunity in front of your customer to extol your own good virtues. Criticizing others creates negative energy and may also paint a negative picture of you as a petty or vindictive or jealous person, which in turn reflects on your business. It makes you look bad in the long run and not necessarily your competition. There is no place for it.

When my partner and I opened our first business, we were very small. We had to work out of the warehouse in our new building until our offices were finished, and so we had to start off in a humble working space. As far as our clients went, we were dealing with some of the biggest firms in the industry. They were big deals with big personalities to match. Therefore, because of our size, there was a massive amount of negativity directed at us by our competitors. Unfortunately for them, our company may have been small at the start but our outstanding reputation was very large. The bad things they had to say about us hurt them more.

We were smart; we never reacted nor countered. We never complained, and we never wasted time talking about others. We decided, as a team, that we would be the "bigger" company; we were too busy focusing on our own signature and "quietly making noise." We spent our valuable time speaking about our products and the service we could provide, as well as proving ourselves to our customers. Time and time again, we substantiated who we were and did not show glory in our competitors' failures.

Be decent people and make a decent business.

6. *How do you do your homework?*

In order to do homework, ask your customers, this includes future ones as well, what they want. Ask them for their thoughts and opinions on your branding, your hours, and your offerings. Find and collect data to make your next move. Each move that you make should move you closer to a future where your business succeeds.

7. *What is the link between customer service and sales and marketing?*

Customer service relates to sales and marketing in countless ways. Customer service agents are important participants in the dance of your business because they have direct relationships with the customers. They have insights that others in your business may not have access to. For that reason, customer service agents must pass on information about repeated problems, repeated success, and repeated requests, as well as anything else that is specific in importance to your product or service regarding sales.

Essentially, customer service agents are the voice of the customer. Take, for instance, my "build your own salad" anecdote earlier in the chapter. We marketed to and sold our customers on this new service, and they gave our customer service representatives solid feedback. By giving your customers a voice through your service agents, you are allowing your customers to feel important. This importance, in turn, gives them the power to be proactive, not reactive. Being proactive allows the shopkeeper to move forward toward innovation and creativity. This is essentially what happened when I was offered the personal concierge service from my earlier story. I was given a means by which I could voice all my needs and opinions at any time through a single easy forum, and they now have the opportunity to give habits and patterns, as well as a wealth of information and comments, back to sales and marketing.

8. *Why is the power of product not enough for most companies?*

Products don't sell themselves for you. Giants are extreme cases; you can't rely on the name and/or advertising to hold sales up. You also need the power of a beautifully trained staff.

9. *How does follow-up apply to training?*

Follow-up is an important aspect to offering great customer service. It should never be left out of training and should never be unmonitored. Don't let a complaint go unserviced.

10. *What do you do if you've done everything but it's not working?*

First, take stock of the whole staff—from the service people up to the shopkeeper. Ask yourself what the promise of the business is. Did you make sure to explain to everyone what the goal is? Did you outline that goal appropriately? Did you give yourself enough time to reach said goal?

Get on the floor and ask, "OK, who's putting on the 'chicken suit'"? By "chicken suit" I am referring to that person dressed up as a chicken and standing on the street corner with a hard to miss sign that says, "Factory Blowout Sale" or "Best Burgers in Town," who is trying to drive customer traffic. Everyone should wear the metaphorical chicken suit to attract customers. Look to everyone for ideas.

Perhaps something needs to be fixed. Were you ready for opening? If not, you will for sure know right away. You may not have been as ready as you wanted to be right off the bat. Does your product or service need tweaking? Is it reaching your target, or do you need to redefine that?

**11.** *What should you do if you have to cut back on the service or product you offer?*

Let the customers know if changes in your business are going to affect them. Hopefully, if things go south and you have to accommodate for cutbacks, you can have it appear as if you are making moves because it is for the best interest of the customer. Be creative in how you tell customers about changes, but you must tell them. If you don't let your customers know about price hikes, or dropped products or services, your staff will feel the heat when the customers get angry.

**12.** *Keep dancing and keep the music going.*

I always have music playing in my businesses, because I want the dance to always be going on. For Millennials, music is important. Music keeps your business atmosphere light and everyone on their feet. It's okay to turn it up and let it go sometimes.

On a final note, I want to spend a moment reflecting back. My airport has changed recently, including remodelling and restructuring the whole process of customs and security. It really does function more appropriately, and there are less bottlenecks, albeit so far. We are progressing, moving with the times, and becoming more efficient. But they are gone, those two lovely people I looked forward to seeing on my way through. That area has been closed off, taken down, and cleaned up, all in the name of progress. I hope they have been given or found a place to continue their excellent service. Why wouldn't they have?

I have recently spent a considerable amount of time flying a regular route, with the same airline, several times a month. It is not a large plane, and the trip takes only a few hours. There were always two cold meal choices, but both contained meat, which I usually don't eat. One day, as I was about to decline as usual, the now-familiar steward proudly displayed a single vegetarian meal option. I smiled, thanked him graciously, did not tell him I had just eaten at the airport, and accepted the tray. Because I am a good customer.

# ACKNOWLEDGMENTS

I would like to acknowledge the most wonderful people who have been a part of this, mostly for the listening but definitely for the sharing of stories and laughter. To Barbara Boyd and especially to Meghan Fitzpatrick without whom the book wouldn't have proceeded and who definitely became more "sensitive" to service. It was a joy to work with you both. To Jennifer Ferguson and Patricia Nelson for their limitless amount of enthusiasm for whatever I endeavour. To Suzy, Amanda, and Serafina for trusting me and never failing to give their absolute best to their customers. To Nicole and Michael for their love and support, always. To Susan O'Brien, the Wilma to my Betty. To Charles Leriche for his kindness while going above and beyond in service, you will go far my friend. And, lastly, to my publisher Holly Foreman for patiently hearing my voice.

# ABOUT THE AUTHOR

**SHARI MOSS** spent the first twenty years of her career climbing the ladder in customer service, growing from direct client care to VP of Sales, and all the way to Business Owner in Telecom. Along the way she mastered the ability to read and impress clients with timeless tactics, which served her well when launching her own businesses in the culinary world. She now dances between those successful businesses, publishing, and her work in film production. Shari splits time between Toronto, Austin, and a magical place somewhere on the Great Lakes with her two children and the family dog Jake. Read more about Shari's endeavours on her blog at **www.shariannemoss.com**, and contact her at **shopkeeper@sharimoss.ca**.